Race and Crime

PATTERSON SMITH REPRINT SERIES IN
CRIMINOLOGY, LAW ENFORCEMENT, AND SOCIAL PROBLEMS

1. Lewis: *The Development of American Prisons and Prison Customs, 1776-1845*
2. Carpenter: *Reformatory Prison Discipline*
3. Brace: *The Dangerous Classes of New York*
4. Dix: *Remarks on Prisons and Prison Discipline in the United States*
5. Bruce *et al: The Workings of the Indeterminate-Sentence Law and the Parole System in Illinois*
6. Wickersham Commission: *Complete Reports, Including the Mooney-Billings Report.* 14 Vols.
7. Livingston: *Complete Works on Criminal Jurisprudence.* 2 Vols.
8. Cleveland Foundation: *Criminal Justice in Cleveland*
9. Illinois Association for Criminal Justice: *The Illinois Crime Survey*
10. Missouri Association for Criminal Justice: *The Missouri Crime Survey*
11. Aschaffenburg: *Crime and Its Repression*
12. Garofalo: *Criminology*
13. Gross: *Criminal Psychology*
14. Lombroso: *Crime, Its Causes and Remedies*
15. Saleilles: *The Individualization of Punishment*
16. Tarde: *Penal Philosophy*
17. McKelvey: *American Prisons*
18. Sanders: *Negro Child Welfare in North Carolina*
19. Pike: *A History of Crime in England.* 2 Vols.
20. Herring: *Welfare Work in Mill Villages*
21. Barnes: *The Evolution of Penology in Pennsylvania*
22. Puckett: *Folk Beliefs of the Southern Negro*
23. Fernald *et al: A Study of Women Delinquents in New York State*
24. Wines: *The State of the Prisons and of Child-Saving Institutions*
25. Raper: *The Tragedy of Lynching*
26. Thomas: *The Unadjusted Girl*
27. Jorns: *The Quakers as Pioneers in Social Work*
28. Owings: *Women Police*
29. Woolston: *Prostitution in the United States*
30. Flexner: *Prostitution in Europe*
31. Kelso: *The History of Public Poor Relief in Massachusetts: 1820-1920*
32. Spivak: *Georgia Nigger*
33. Earle: *Curious Punishments of Bygone Days*
34. Bonger: *Race and Crime*
35. Fishman: *Crucibles of Crime*
36. Brearley: *Homicide in the United States*
37. Graper: *American Police Administration*
38. Hichborn: *"The System"*
39. Steiner & Brown: *The North Carolina Chain Gang*
40. Cherrington: *The Evolution of Prohibition in the United States of America*
41. Colquhoun: *A Treatise on the Commerce and Police of the River Thames*
42. Colquhoun: *A Treatise on the Police of the Metropolis*
43. Abrahamsen: *Crime and the Human Mind*
44. Schneider: *The History of Public Welfare in New York State: 1609-1866*
45. Schneider & Deutsch: *The History of Public Welfare in New York State: 1867-1940*
46. Crapsey: *The Nether Side of New York*
47. Young: *Social Treatment in Probation and Delinquency*
48. Quinn: *Gambling and Gambling Devices*
49. McCord & McCord: *Origins of Crime*
50. Worthington & Topping: *Specialized Courts Dealing with Sex Delinquency*

PUBLICATION NO. 34: PATTERSON SMITH REPRINT SERIES IN
CRIMINOLOGY, LAW ENFORCEMENT, AND SOCIAL PROBLEMS

Race and Crime

By WILLEM ADRIAAN BONGER

Translated from the Dutch by
MARGARET MATHEWS HORDYK

Montclair, New Jersey
PATTERSON SMITH
1969

SBN 87585-034-0

Library of Congress Catalog Card Number: 69-14912

Willem Adriaan Bonger

ON MAY 15, 1940, the distinguished Professor Bonger, of the University of Amsterdam, passed away. He was the prime leader in criminology in the Netherlands, successor in eminence to George van Hamel, one of the great triumvirate who founded the International Association of Criminology more than half a century ago.

He was born on September 16, 1876, and graduated at the University of Amsterdam in 1905; he specialized from the first in criminal sociology with a dissertation on *Criminality and Economic Conditions*. This monograph was enlarged into a treatise and was published in the United States in 1916 in an English translation as a volume in the Modern Criminal Science Series, under the auspices of the Association of American Law Schools (Boston, Little Brown & Co.).

The author was married in 1905 to Marie Hendrika van Heteren. From 1905 to 1922 he was director of an insurance association. Meanwhile he continued his researches and publications in criminology: *Evolution and Revolution* (1919), *Property and Income in War-Time* (1923), and numerous periodical articles.

In 1922 he was appointed Professor of Sociology and Criminology at the University of Amsterdam, and held this position until his decease. Meantime he was active nationally in many aspects of practical science, founder of the Netherlands Sociological Association; Editor in Chief from 1915 of the *Sociological Guide;* Editor of *Men and Society* (the

Dutch sociological review); member of the Central Statistical Bureau, the Psychopathic Council, the Economic Council, and the Netherlands Railway Board. In 1934 he published *Religion and Irreligion in the Netherlands,* and in 1933 the crowning results of his life study: *Inleiding tot de criminologie,* 1932, of which the English translation, *Introduction to Criminology,* was published in London, 1936. The present work, a translation of *Ras en Misdaad* (Haarlem, 1939), is a revealing study of statistics showing the relative behavior of race stocks.

Among the criminologists of the passing generation he stands out as a preëminent specialist in the sound analysis of statistics, and the leading exponent of the philosophy of crime as a social and not a biological phenomenon.

JOHN H. WIGMORE

Translator's Note

IN HOLLAND most of the universities are closed. The professors are not permitted to speak. Many have gone; they are in the concentration camps, or have died of grief, of shock, of mistreatment, or of their own free will. Professor Bonger was among the latter. Such a man could never live in a world where he was not free to be honest and to express scientific truths.

The break in the continuity of European scholarship which is being caused by the war is a deep tragedy. After the war we shall need all the vision and straight thinking we can muster, in order to organize a better world. Nothing can ever fill the place of the European professors who have gone, and the generation of young people whose universities have been closed will be immeasurably poorer for having lacked contact with them.

Our work here in America is now one of salvage. We must keep the international aspects and the continuity of science alive. Just as we receive refugee scholars and find places for them among us, so we can sometimes receive refugee books, and, by translating them, help to keep alive the continuity of human thought.

This was Professor Bonger's final book, and it was one of his last expressed wishes to have it appear in English. I received it during the very week of the invasion of Holland, in May 1940—a veritable orphan on my doorstep. And since it represents a contribution to our future, better world, and a discarding of old prejudices, I humbly undertook to translate it.

Though I began with a feeling that I was ill prepared for the task, I soon discovered that Professor Bonger's writing was so clear and logical that the work was a pleasure. Now that it is completed, I take pride in having made this small contribution to the study of man.

I am very grateful to Professor John Wigmore, of Northwestern University, for his kindly interest and encouragement throughout my undertaking, and for his contribution of the Biographical Note, which originally appeared in the *Journal of Criminal Law and Criminology* for March–April, 1941. My sincere thanks go to Dr. Bartholomew Landheer for reading my manuscript, to the Netherlands Information Bureau for making possible its publication, and to my husband, Gerard Hordyk, whose help was of inestimable value during the progress of the work.

MARGARET MATHEWS HORDYK

New York
December, 1942

Author's Foreword

To UNDERTAKE writing at present on the connection between race and crime seems like a hopeless task. Never has a doctrine fallen so into disrepute as that of race. Pettiness and lunacy dominate the whole subject. No trace of science remains. Bestial passions and baseless prejudices have led to situations which but a short time ago would have been considered totally impossible. In certain countries the Jews are robbed and mistreated in hundreds of thousands. They are killed or driven out for no other reason than that they differ anthropologically from the rest of the population. A part of mankind has fallen back to the level of those Middle Ages when just such a primitive irrationality was uppermost in men's minds. But this is much more dangerous now than it formerly was, for now men have the means of modern technique and publicity at their disposal.

One might therefore be tempted to throw the whole race doctrine into the discard and to return to the old point of view according to which men of all races are spiritually the same. (The physical differences of all races are visible to everyone and are thus undeniable.) Yet in so doing one would not advance matters in the least, but rather retreat several steps, since this former point of view was not based on investigation but was dogmatic.

In a scientific publication on race and crime it is best simply to ignore the present senseless race prejudice. It is a social-pathological phenomenon which is in itself in need of explaining, but which is of no importance for other problems. For one who knows himself to be free from every race prejudice, and for whom to be different by no means implies to be inferior or still less to be hostile, there is, as I see it, no objection to examining the problem in question, *sine ira et studio.*

The intention of this study is to review critically the present state of affairs. There is no promise—here we already anticipate one of the conclusions—of reaching definite results. On the contrary, it will appear that much on this subject is uncertain and that much is left for future researchers. To note this condition is also worth while in science.

W. A. BONGER

June, 1939

Contents

Willem Adriaan Bonger *by John H. Wigmore*   v

Translator's Note   vii

Author's Foreword   ix

I.   Introduction. On Race in General   1

II.   Race and Crime. General Considerations   18

    History   18

    Theory   27

III.   Race and Crime. Case Studies   42

    Negro Criminality   42

    Jewish Criminality   51

    Mediterranean Criminality   66

    Alpine Criminality   76

    The Criminality of the Nordics   86

    The Criminality of the Ugro-Finns   90

    The Criminality of the East Baltics and Others   97

IV.   Résumé and Conclusion   103

    Bibliography   109

    Index   125

CHAPTER I

Introduction

ON RACE IN GENERAL

THE PROBLEM of defining "a race" belongs to the subject of anthropology [1] and must be left to students of that science. However, it appears on examination that the terminology of this problem is not altogether fixed. Pittard agrees with Boule, who gives the following definition: "By race should be understood the continuity of a physical type, carrying over inherited conformities, representing a purely natural grouping. It has not necessarily and not generally to do with artificial groupings such as peoples, nationalities, language, or customs, for these are not at all anthropological and only spring from history, whose products they are." [2] In his *Les Races et les peuples de la terre* (2d ed., 1926) Deniker says: "The word race is nearly universally used today to designate the various physical types of humanity . . ." According to him one could also speak of subspecies; and there would appear to be no essential difference between race, subspecies, and species. Weidenreich gives the following definition: "By race . . . is understood a group of people who are distinguished from others by the common possession

[1] In accordance with present scientific terminology, anthropology refers only to physical anthropology, the subject of which is physical man. Consequently it is a natural science. Man as a social being is the subject of ethnology, sociology, and history.

[2] Marcellin Boule's definition, as quoted by Pittard in *Les Races et l'histoire*, p. 4.

of certain hereditary characteristics." [3] According to Frets, a race is distinguished "by similarity of qualities—a group of qualities by which it is distinguished from other races of mankind. A race is distinguished from a species in that individuals from different species when mating generally produce no offspring; crossing is not possible." [4] To conclude, here is a citation from the most recent Netherlands work on the race problem, by Barge: "Race is a group of human individuals distinguished from other similar groups by the common possession of a number of inheritable physical characteristics." [5]

Biological terminology, touched upon by Deniker among others, need no longer occupy us in a study such as the present one. Nor need we study the problem of the origin of the races. One of the races, for instance, may have been the original one (monogenic theory) from which the others have sprung, or the various races may have come into being at the same time (polygenic theory). There seems to be no agreement among the anthropologists on this question. They seem at present to incline toward the monogenic theory. The question as to where the genus Homo sapiens first made his appearance on the earth is irrelevant to our problem. (Here also there is no uniformity of opinion; the anthropologists seem inclined to consider Central Asia as his original home.)

Thus the essential points in the definition are (1) a number of characteristics in common, and (2) their inherita-

[3] "Die physischen Grundlagen der Rassenlehre," in *Rasse und Geist*, pp. 5–6.

[4] *Erfelijkheid*, pp. 213–14.

[5] S. R. Steinmetz, J. A. J. Barge, A. L. Hagedorn, and R. Steinmetz, *De Rassen der Menschheid*, pp. 3–4. In the same year there also appeared a concise little work, *Het Rassenvraagstuk*, by Dr. G. W. Kastein.

bility.[6] It is of the greatest importance to emphasize the second point explicitly. Without this inheritability one cannot speak of race. If, and in so far as, crime and race are connected, then this connection is inheritable.

By what physical characteristics do the anthropologists distinguish the races of man? By the pigmentation of skin, eyes, and hair; type of hair; skull index; length of body; and by certain characteristics of physiognomy (nose and lip formation). On these grounds they have come to very divergent numbers of races, varying from three to twenty-nine (Deniker). We find the earliest research workers using the classification into three (white, yellow, black). After holding many different opinions, research workers have again returned to this classification.[7] These are the principal races, which may again be divided into a number of subraces.[8]

If a remark on this classification may be permitted from a layman, then it is this: these distinctions are rather "superficial." They are not based, for instance, on the skeleton as a whole, or on the finer structure of the brain, but on the color of the skin, and so forth.[9] If all peoples had the same skin color, for instance, there would not be much of the whole

[6] The word "race" can mean something quite different in biology. Take, for example, the meaning expressed in the words "race hygiene" and "eugenics." This hygiene attempts to hinder the propagation of unfavorable variants and to further the propagation of favorable ones. Here the variability stands in the foreground, with the degree to which this is inheritable (tendency to inheritability). In our study we shall not deal with this question.

[7] For the history of the classification of the races of man, see Scheidt, *Allgemeine Rassenkunde*, pp. 1 ff. In Bijlmer's *Rassen en Kruisingen* (Erfelijkheid bij de Mens IV) one may find a sketch of this history.

[8] Among others we find a detailed description in the previously mentioned study by Barge.

[9] On this see Deniker, *Les Races et les peuples de la terre*, 2d ed., pp. 102 ff.

classification left over. By so saying one does not mean naturally that no deeper differences will come to light in the future, but that at present the classification is rather "superficial." Whoever would form an idea of the relative slightness of these variations should think, for example, of the enormous differences in the races of dogs which are utterly divergent in appearance, for example, King Charles and German police dog. On the other hand, where men are concerned one also takes for granted that they speak the same language, wear the same clothes, and have the same customs and manners, and so forth, all of which have nothing to do with race. One may then easily conclude that if the "superficial" differences were absent the countless laymen and amateurs who now get so excited over race problems would give them hardly any attention, and that the whole question would be treated exclusively by the group of professional anthropologists.

Finally, we should like to point out that all races can learn all languages, and that all races can reproduce when crossbred. This is so much the case that crossbreeding between the principal races occurs frequently, and among the subraces it occurs to such an extent that some anthropologists almost deny the existence of race purity. This, however, is considered an exaggeration by the majority of authors. Besides the numerous mixed races there are others which are still pure.

What we have been discussing until now has to do exclusively with the physical qualities of races. This side of the problem, however, is without any importance in the question of the relationship between race and crime. It is completely indifferent to the criminologist whether the criminal is tall or short, has a round or a long skull, is black or white. In criminology it is only a question of the psychical. And now the difficulties really begin.

Whoever examines the question of the psychical differences among races accepts the fact that genus Homo sapiens forms a unit primarily and fundamentally independent of race. All men of all races are driven by the same motives; the same feelings and passions are common to all. Nor do men differ from sensory or motor points of view.[10] Just as all races are capable of reproducing when crossbred, they are also psychically very close to each other. "Ahead of all race characteristics go the generally valid spiritual characteristics of men.[11] . . . The general spiritual processes, the perceptions and conceptions, the sentiments and impulses of the will of men have remained the same through all time, not only in their formal qualities but also in the general condition of their origin and content." [12]

Numerous conclusions of this kind could be quoted.[13] I shall limit myself to those of the Netherlands explorer Bijlmer in his recent work, *Naar de Achterhoek der Aarde* (1928), in which he reports on his expeditions to Central New Guinea, the home of the dwarf Papuans. These belong to the most primitive of peoples. They still live in the Stone Age; their race differs more from ours than does any other. Dr. Bijlmer says:

They are real persons. According to circumstances they are friendly or cross, meek or obstinate, diligent or lazy, enterpris-

[10] On this point see Garth, *Race Psychology*, chap. iii.
[11] Wundt, *Völkerpsychologie*, VII, 48.   [12] *Ibid.*, p. 51.
[13] Oppenheimer has brought a number of opinions together in his *System der Soziologie*, I, 213 ff.

ing or leisurely, and their reaction is precisely that which we are accustomed to observe in our fellow men. In questions of law and lawlessness, loyalty and disloyalty, or, to state it generally, in interpretations of justice they have the same conception that we have. Our words mean little to each other because of the difference in language, but with our thoughts we understand each other as noble creatures of the same order.[14]

Centuries of culture separate us, but the breach thus created affects the intrinsic values but little. It becomes clear to me how artificial our conceptions of prehistory are. How little we are aware that the Europeans of the Stone Age, thousands and thousands of years ago, were probably just ordinary people.[15]

Although the races may not differ fundamentally from a psychical point of view, this naturally indicates nothing on the subject of their quantitative differences, which may be very important. Races differ from a physical point of view but that is no indication that they differ psychically, although it makes it probable. Modern research (especially that of such men as MacAuliffe and Kretschmer) on the connection between physical build and character makes this admissible.[16]

Granting, now, that the psychical disposition of races differs, one can think of this difference in two ways. (1) Either a certain quality is to be found in one race while it is entirely lacking in another, or (2) the distribution of this quality is not equal: for example, in one race a greater percentage of artistically inclined persons will appear than in another. This, then, following the law of individual differences, will also mean that the average level of artistic disposi-

[14] Page 77.   [15] Page 86.
[16] Kretschmer points out that his constitution types do not coincide with races. They appear in all races. (See "Genie und Rasse," in *Rasse und Geist,* p. 60.)

tion is higher in the first race than in the second. To express it in terms of statistics, the two curves in which the quality in question is numerically expressed partially overlap (so-called "overlapping curves"). It may be taken as certain that the second theory is the correct one—it is to the credit of Steinmetz that he first pointed this out.[17] There are no races completely devoid of any given quality of a psychical nature. In physical matters it is otherwise: brunette and blond do not blend. When one says, for example, that the Nordics are phlegmatic, it only means that the percentage of phlegmatic persons among them is greater than among the Mediter-raneans, where the type also exists.

Having spoken of possibilities, let us now speak of facts. First we ask what the anthropologists have to say on racial differences in psychical qualities. The answers are not en-couraging. Deniker says: "It is highly probable that psychi-cal activity is in certain relationship to race, but until the present time this has not been scientifically proved." [18] Wei-denreich does not deny the possibility of variations but adds: "There is no sure method of comprehending the primary, universal, spiritual qualities of a race, and at the same time eliminating everything which can be ascribed to environ-ment, tradition, experience, imitation, and above all to pure individual talent." [19] Barge finds it a priori just as little certain that there should exist no variations with regard to the spirit. "The establishment of this as a fact, however, demands an

[17] In his "Der erbliche Rassen- und Volkscharakter," in *Gesammelte kleinere Schriften zur Ethnologie und Soziologie,* II (formerly appeared in *Vierteljahrsschrift für wissenschaftliche Philosophie und Soziologie,* 1902).
[18] *Les Races et les peuples de la terre,* p. 149.
[19] *Rasse und Geist,* p. 20.

investigation directed especially toward this end, and such an investigation has not, or at least not sufficiently, been made. The classifying of races as we know it from physical anthropology is based on physical distinctions and on these alone. The spiritual qualities are not investigated together with the physical ones." [20] The writer points out in conclusion that even if a race should seem to have certain spiritual qualities it would still be doubtful whether these would be recognizable as such, since these qualities depend not only on physical race distinctions but also on a number of other factors (physical milieu, economic relations, and so forth).

The earlier anthropology—especially of such amateur anthropologists as Vacher de Lapouge and Ammon—made it easier for itself than does the present. When the classification between dolichocephalic and brachycephalic was made, the long-skulled people were promoted to the ranks of the intelligent. Now that it has appeared that the Negroes are dolichocephalic and that many talented and genial people are brachycephalic, this assertion has been denied.[21] At that time it was also thought that the cranial capacity—as an indication of the weight of the brain—was a determining factor in the question. In general this theory has also been relegated to the land of fables. "The degree of intellect cannot be reckoned by mathematics, nor can the height of culture be read from the cubic centimeter measure of a slide rule." [22] Primitive races sometimes have large cranial capacities (the Eskimos, for example), and geniuses sometimes have small ones. In general, however, intellectually gifted persons have larger

[20] *De Rassen der Menschheid*, p. 4.
[21] See, for example, Weidenreich, *Rasse und Geist*, p. 23.
[22] *Ibid.*, p. 21.

head sizes, which probably only indicates that their brains have grown in a good normal way.

Intellectual capacity does not depend on the quantity but on the quality of the brain, as even the layman can surmise.[23] Why shouldn't the quality contribute to the finest and noblest instrument? Weidenreich says: "We know that it is not a question of the mass of the brain, but of the quality of the surface configuration and still more of the fineness of the cortex." [24]

Is enough known then (and this is what it comes to from an anthropological point of view) about the finer structure of the brain in the different races? We must answer in the negative. Boas observes in his *Kultur und Rasse* (1914): "In spite of many attempts to find in the finer structure of the brains of different races distinctions which may be directly connected with psychological differences, no convincing evidences that these exist have until now been offered." [25]

The individual differences between members of the same race are so great that those between races themselves are small by comparison.

[23] Only fools would deny that there is a connection between brains and spirit. There is much disagreement over the nature of this connection. This is, however, a philosophical question which need not be considered here.

[24] *Rasse und Geist*, p. 22.

[25] Deniker writes in the same spirit, *Les Races et les peuples de la terre*, pp. 120–22. Hankins calls attention to a comparative study of the brain structure of whites and Negroes which would seem to prove the inferiority of the latter (*The Racial Basis of Civilization*, p. 317). In order to have some certainty on this important point, I asked the opinion of one of Holland's foremost authorities, Professor Arriëns Kappers. He assured me that this sort of study is only in its inception, and nothing positive can be said of it. A competent anthropologist is not capable of distinguishing from among a number of human brains which come from whites and which from Negroes.

Historians have followed quite a different road in trying
to prove that the psychical disposition of the races differs,
and that this difference is the cause of their adventures and
their present place in human society. In calling these investi-
gators historians one generally honors them too much:
pseudo historians would be a better name for them. Their
method, moreover, is quite different from the one spoken of
above. They start from the viewpoint that the white race is
the most gifted, the black race the least so, and try to prove
this by history. Of the white race, then, the Nordic (Homo
nordicus) would be the most exceptional, to be credited with
just about all that is good and beautiful in mankind. This
race, according to them, should be the decisive factor in history.

The list of these authors is headed by Gobineau, *Essai sur
l'inégalité des races humaines* (1853), and extends by way of
Houston Stewart Chamberlain, *Die Grundlagen des XIX
Jahrhunderts* (1899); Vacher de Lapouge, *L'Aryen; son
rôle social* (1899); Woltmann, *Politische Anthropologie*
(1903); Madison Grant, *The Passing of the Great Race*
(1916); to Günther, *Rassenkunde des deutschen Volkes*
(1922). The lesser gods who have followed these writers
are numerous.[26] Their theory originated in France, where,
however, it never had an important following. It has taken
hold especially in Germany and also to a certain extent in
America. Since the Nazi regime this race doctrine has been
developed especially along anti-Semitic lines.

If one asks whether these partisans are even partially suc-
cessful in proving their thesis, then the answer must be a

[26] It hardly needs to be said that they are often in disagreement with
each other.

decided No. It is really no theory at all but a second-rate religion. Things are not proved but only alleged. It resembles the commonly witnessed phenomenon of persons who, quite without reason, fancy themselves (and often their families also) to be more exalted than others. But now it is carried out on a much larger scale, and with much greater detriment to society, since it affects wide-spread groups.

There is no place here to criticize the theory extensively. We shall name some of the most important critics: it is interesting to note that they are nearly all professionals, while the race theorists are amateurs. We call attention to Manouvrier, "L'Indice céphalique et la pseudo-sociologie" (*Revue de l'École d'Anthropologie*, 1899); Ripley, *The Races of Europe* (standard work); Steinmetz, *Der erbliche Rassen- und Volkscharakter* (1902); Hertz, *Moderne Rassentheorien* (1904); Houzé, *L'Aryen et l'anthroposociologie* (1906); Oppenheimer, *Die rassentheoretische Geschichtsphilosophie* (1912); Boas, *Kultur und Rasse* (1914); Pittard, *Les Races et l'histoire* (1924); and Hankins, *Racial Basis of Civilization* (1926).

Historians are concerned with people who come either from different races or from crossbreeding and who seldom consist of a pure race. Historians deal with events which arise from character—the great unknown—and environment, to which belongs the power of tradition. Some go so far as to ignore completely the importance of the race in the course of history. Goetz says: "Environment and historical development form the peoples no matter from what race they descend." [27] Others, while not denying the possibility of the influence of race, cannot demonstrate it and ask the anthro-

[27] "Rasse und Geschichte," in *Rasse und Geist*, p. 77.

pologist in vain to explain which racial differences are inherited.[28]

Sociologists are, if possible, even more reserved on the race problem. Opposing the general and everywhere prevalent opinion still clung to by the "man in the street" ("He is just born that way," they say), that inherited factors control the course of events, they have demonstrated in long and labored works that circumstances whose importance was never before guessed are of an overwhelming significance. The same regularity in community events is demonstrated by them to exist among all races.[29]

Nothing has worked so strongly in favor of the reserve shown by historians and sociologists as the apparent psychical changeableness in a single race—the so-called spiritual plasticity of the race. Some physical traits are also changeable—length of body, for example—but then only within certain limits. (The Nordics remain taller on the average than the Mediterraneans.) Other traits, however, do not change—for example, the color of the eyes. But the spiritual qualities are extremely variable within one race. To state it more clearly: the possibilities in human talents are very numerous. It depends on circumstances which of these possibilities develop and which ones remain undeveloped and therefore appear not to exist. "Every creature," says Jennings, "has many inheritances, which one shall be realized depending upon the conditions under which it develops; but man is the creature

[28] Note with what great reserve such a man as Bernheim expresses himself (*Lehrbuch der historischen Methode und der Geschichtsphilosophie*, pp. 638 ff.).

[29] Among the best sociological critics of the race theory are: Ripley, *The Races of Europe*, chap. xix, and Ginsberg, *Sociology*, chap. iii. Durkheim, in *Le Suicide*, Livre I, chap. ii, is also especially noteworthy.

that has the greatest number of possible heritages." [30] Peters says:

The evolved characteristics of intelligence and other psychical qualities are not inherited; talent is. The helping and hindering factors in the environment give the measure in which qualities are developed from the talents. The talents can be developed by the environment in various degrees and to some extent probably in various ways. Their development occurs in the tendency to adjust to the persons of the environment and to adapt to the exigencies of the environment.[31]

Examples of this are numerous. Cases in point are: the changeable degree of aggressiveness as shown in the will to make war,[32] or the spirit of enterprise in which the Netherlanders, in comparison with race groups who have remained unified, are one of the typical examples. Compare, for instance, the seventeenth century in the Netherlands with the second half of the eighteenth, and the beginning of the nineteenth with the end. As Müller-Lyer expresses it: "In the spiritual quality of men, the cultural level is of much greater importance than the race." [33]

Plastic as the human spirit may be, this is still no indication that all races have the same potentialities in their talents. This remains an open question. Max Weber, in the "Vorbemerkung" to his *Gesammelte Aufsätze zur Religionssoziologie* (1920), has surveyed the present and future of the question. After saying that he himself is inclined to estimate highly the importance of the inherent factor, he goes on to say:

[30] Cited by Garth, *Race Psychology*, p. 215.
[31] "Rassenpsychologie," in *Rasse und Geist*, p. 55.
[32] In my "De Oorlog als sociologisch Probleem," *Socialistische Gids*, XV (also published separately), I have made some remarks on the subject.
[33] *Der Sinn des Lebens und die Wissenschaft*, p. 180.

Still I can see at present no possible way—in spite of the important accomplishments of anthropological work—of comprehending exactly or surmising their share in the development here being examined.

It should be one of the projects of sociological and historical work to discover as soon as possible all those influences and chains of cause and effect which are to be satisfactorily explained through reactions to destiny and environment. Only then—and when comparative race neurology and race psychology have advanced beyond their present (and occasionally promising) beginnings—may one dare hope perhaps for satisfactory results for this problem also.[34]

Lastly, let us speak of psychology. By this we naturally mean the scientific, experimental variety, and not that of the tourist or of the "man in the street" who says that Americans think only of money, that Frenchmen are nervous scolds, Englishmen phlegmatic, Germans thorough, and so forth.[35]

It is this race psychology which, next to the anatomy of the brain, promises the most for the future, and it can already boast of some results.[36] Psychology unaided is not in a state to eliminate the influence of the milieu. Indeed it cannot approach the soul directly; it can only interpret its expressions psychologically. In these expressions the influence of the milieu (present and past) is contained. By its experimental nature, however, psychology is theoretically in a better state than any other science—except anatomy of the brain—to

[34] Pages 15–16 (edition of 1934).

[35] That such superficialities are not limited to "observers" of that kind, but also appear in the works of serious scientific men, is shown in Fouillée's *Tempérament et caractère*, Livre IV, and Schmoller, *Grundriss der allgemeinen Volkswirtschaftslehre*, I, 141 ff. (edition of 1923).

[36] It was applied about fifty years ago for the first time, but it has been more or less organized only during the last twenty-five years. See Garth, *Race Psychology*, pp. 233 ff.

eliminate the influence of environment. Nevertheless, this laboratory experiment remains a very limited thing, with which biologists, for example, would not be satisfied. If it were possible to handle people like plants or guinea pigs, then experiments could be made in a big way. For example: a thousand Italian babies could be put into English cradles and vice versa, and this exchange could likewise be made between all the races and subraces. Only in such a way could one avoid the mistakes which occur in the examination of individuals of one race who grew up in another milieu.[37] The Italian children would naturally grow up to be English-speaking, Protestant, conservative or enterprising according to the milieu—outwardly English, with all the conceptions and peculiarities of that people; and with the English babies it would be just the opposite. As far as the sociological element goes, there is no question as to the results. For race psychology, however, the problem is whether in these English of Italian origin there would still be noticeable psychological differences, for example, in temperament. The possibility of this is not to be denied, but it is not a certainty.[38]

[37] Steinmetz reports in his study (*Der erbliche Rassen- und Volks-charakter*) on the case of a child from Tierra del Fuego, who after being brought up in England, returned to his native land and in a short time again became a "savage" (p. 259). That, for me, proves nothing for the hypothesis that the "savageness" is inherent. It would prove something only if the child had been brought up from birth in England and then wanted to go back to Tierra del Fuego. And what does one case prove? Steinmetz himself gives a number of facts concerning the possibilities of educating primitives and he concludes: "dass die Naturvölker ursprünglich genau so gutes Menschenmaterial besassen als die Ahnen der Kulturvölker" (p. 265).

[38] The very general opinion that temperament on the whole is not influenced by environment is, certainly, not true where the secondary function is concerned. Otherwise why should the English pay so much attention to self-control in their education (e.g., in sport)? One who

The most extensive and important investigations in the field of race psychology are carried out in the United States. Garth's *Race Psychology*, already mentioned, has a bibliography of nearly two hundred items. Eminent psychologists, such as the German Peters, refer principally to American data.[39] The reasons for this—apart from the enormous means at the disposal of American science—are evident: the United States is a reservoir of numerous and very different races, and there is an intense interest in the problem (limitation of immigration, and so forth). The necessity of separating the man-power according to temperament which was felt when America was obliged to raise an army during the First World War has incidentally contributed to race psychology.

In what departments of the human spirit have these investigations taken place? (The methods used lie too far outside our subject to be treated here.) [40] Research has been pursued in the sphere of artistic disposition (feeling for color and musicality), mental fatigue, temperament, and so forth, and has given some not uninteresting (temporary) results.[41] The principal thing, however, is the intelligence test, applied to groups in the Army (the so-called Army tests) and also given individually by numerous private experimental psy-

visits England is struck by the great reserve in the manner of the Jews, namely those who have grown up in completely English surroundings. See the interesting remarks of McDougall in his *An Introduction to Social Psychology*, pp. 329 f. (16th ed., 1921).

[39] In "Rassenpsychologie," in *Rasse und Geist*.

[40] On this see Peters, in *ibid.*, pp. 38 f. At the Congress of the Institut International d'Anthropologie at Amsterdam in 1927, van Loon and Papillaut reported on the "Organisation de l'étude comparative de la psychologie des races" (*Actes*, pp. 87 f.). Van Loon drew attention to the great importance of psychopathology in this problem.

[41] The work of Garth already mentioned gives the most detailed account of this.

chologists. No results reached have such a degree of probability as those of these Army tests.

Be this as it may, the element of inherent intelligence is of little or no importance in the problem which occupies us at present. Everyday experience teaches us that great intelligence is no guarantee of a good character. In criminology it is an elemental truth that the intelligence is of primary importance in determining the form of the crime, and a restraining influence in the committing of "dumb" crimes. Nothing more. "He has intellect but uses it to be more like an animal than any animal" is the way in which Goethe characterizes man.

Other psychical qualities examined, such as that of artistic feeling, have nothing, on the whole, to add to criminology. At the same time, experiments in personality, which are just what is needed, are only in their very inception.

The situation in scientific race psychology at present is not very encouraging for our problem. We shall thus be forced to turn, for the greater part, to cruder daily observations with all their accompanying unsureness.

CHAPTER II

Race and Crime. General Considerations

HISTORY

W HEN one reviews the history of criminology, one finds
that very little material has been published on the
connection between race and crime, and in general this material is very superficial.

Naturally one might expect that the Anthropological, or
Italian School (which considers that it has found the cause
of crime principally in inherent factors) would give a large
place to the significance of race. This is indeed the case,
though but few writers have expressed themselves on the
subject, and the foundation of their hypothesis is, as usual,
exceedingly weak.

In his *L'uomo delinquente* (1876) Lombroso does not express an opinion on this subject. He first attacks the problem
in *Le Crime; causes et remèdes* (1899). After making some
remarks on crime among primitive peoples, which only give
evidence of the author's lack of ethnological knowledge, he
informs us:

The documents which serve to demonstrate the ethnic influence
on crime in our civilized world are less doubtful. We know that
a large portion of the thieves of London are the sons of the Irish,
or natives of Lancashire. In Russia, writes Anutschine, Bessa-
rabians and Crimeans furnish all the thieves of the capital. In
comparison with the number of arraignments, convictions are
numerically greater among them: criminality is transmitted

from one family to another. (Séance of the Geographical Society, 1868, Saint Petersburg.) In Germany it is recognized that in the sections which have colonies of gypsies there is the greatest tendency to theft by women.[1]

Such assertions are called *less doubtful documents!* Lombroso further asserts that in Sicily highway robbery is concentrated in a strip where the Berbers formerly settled. The fact that in northern Italy aggressive criminality is limited is due to German admixture. In France the dolichocephalic types would appear to show a greater criminality than the brachycephalic ones, and so forth.[2] In short, these are nothing but assertions for which not the slightest evidence, not the slightest explanation, is supplied.

Ferri, in his *Sociologie Criminelle* (1893, first edition in 1884), speaks of race as the anthropological factor in crime, without adding any explanation to the remark.[3]

Garofalo, in his *Criminologie* (1890, first edition in 1885), asserts that on the Aspö Islands near Finland there are descendants of Spanish or Arabic peoples who landed there several centuries ago. These are "always ready to draw their knives."[4] In Austria it seems that the Slavic peoples are inclined to aggressive crime, and in Belgium, the Flemish. No explanation of this is given.

In his *Naturgeschichte des Verbrechers* (1893) Kurella agrees in principle with the above opinion. "Race and nation-

[1] Page 27.
[2] See also Lombroso, *Neue Verbrecherstudien*, pp. 54 ff., which does not contain anything new. Vol. XXIV of the *Archivio di psichiatria, anthropologia criminale e szienzi penale*, should contain a study by Lombroso on "Razze e criminalità in Italia." I have not been able to obtain it. (It is available in the New York Public Library. Translator's note.)
[3] Page 151.   [4] Page 435.

ality are important factors in crime. In them the whole sum
of the inheritance of many generations expresses itself." [5] He
recognizes, however, that the problem is very difficult—for
example where statistics are concerned—and that it is only
possible to determine the importance of the race factor after
a painstaking analysis, since social and physical factors also
play a role here. He attributes the greater aggressive criminality of South Europe to race. Klaatsch, the well-known
German anthropologist, in his paper before the International
Criminal Anthropological Congress at Cologne in 1911, took
a unique position, somewhat reminiscent of Lombroso's theory of atavism. In prehistoric times, he said, Europe was inhabited by two races of men: the Aurignac and the Neanderthal. The second was supplanted by the first, but distant
descendants of the Neanderthal men are still living. The
nature of the Neanderthal was "rough," of the Aurignac,
"noble." "Applied to the population of Europe, the results of
this study indicate that in skeleton and brain the Neanderthal
race belongs to the Western type and the Aurignac peoples to
the Eastern type. Applied to the present, they show that both
types still exist today in the population of Europe, sometimes
separately, sometimes mixed." [6]

Klaatsch offers the hypothesis that the brains of men with
social defects (as criminals) show a relationship to the brains
of the Neanderthal men. Since he offers neither hide nor hair
of proof and, so far as I know, nothing has come out of his

[5] Page 153.
[6] "Die Morphologie und Psychologie der niederen Menschenrassen
in ihrer Bedeutung für die Probleme der Kriminalistik," *Bericht über den
VII Int. Kongr. f. Kriminalanthropologie*, p. 72. See also: "Die niederen
Menschenrassen in ihrer Bedeutung für die Kriminalistik," *Die Umschau*,
XV (1911).

idea (Klaatsch had never specialized in criminology), the hypothesis can be left to slumber.

As one might expect, the harvest from the sociological school is even more meager. Some of this school have expressed themselves, in passing, on the relation of race to crime,[7] but one seldom finds a really profound treatment of the subject. The only author who expresses himself rather fully, in my opinion, is Colajanni, in his *Sociologia criminale*. The essence of his criticism of the race hypothesis lies in this: that very divergent moral and intellectual situations may be observed in the same race, and the same situations are seen in different races. In the field of crime all races show similar habits and the same forms.[8]

Among the bio-sociological writers we find a few who have considered the subject.[9] Aschaffenburg, in his *Das Verbrechen und seine Bekämpfung* (1906, first edition, 1903, third, 1923), begins by recognizing that in this field very little is known. The difference in criminality among the races can often be explained by entirely different factors. The following citation accurately reflects his conclusion:

Apart from the fact that we have not yet gone very far or reached final results in an understanding of races, and that we scarcely find any entirely pure groups at present, the economic conditions of various lands are so different that it is scarcely possible to prove the importance of race differences in criminality.

[7] See, for example, Quetelet, *Physique sociale* (1869), II, 279 ff.; Tarde, *La Philosophic pénale*, pp. 320 ff.; Ettinger, *Das Verbrecherproblem in anthropologischer und sociologischer Beleuchtung*, I, 194 ff.

[8] II, 220 and 305.

[9] Wulffen must also be counted among these. See his *Psychologie des Verbrechers*, I, 311 ff., as well as *Kriminalpsychologie*, pp. 158 ff. As usual, the work of this author contains nothing new.

This does not mean that racial characteristics are without importance for psychology; it requires no serious study of the psychology of nations to recognize the differences between the light, excitable Italians and the cautious Nordics, between the calm, somewhat grave nature of the low Germans, and the joyful, noisy character of the Palatinate.[10]

Although French criminologists generally support the environment theory, Corre must rather be considered as a biosociologist. In his *Crime et suicide* (1891) and *L'Ethnographie criminelle* (1894) he has expressed his opinion on race and crime.[11] "Crime exists among all races. It is neither the exclusive product of any one anatomic form nor of any social form, for it proceeds from instincts common to all men from whatever anthropological stock they spring, and to whatever form of society they belong." [12] As the community develops it sets higher standards with which some individuals (rebellious natures) cannot collaborate. The proportion in which these persons appear in the different races gives the measure of criminality of these races. This, however, is most difficult to establish, since the influence of the physical and social milieus also counts for something. "But some part of the original stock is always preserved. New physical qualities, new tendencies and aptitudes come to graft themselves little by little: a sum of qualities and defects, resistances and predispositions to abnormality become fixed in a type that grows fairly independent of his own milieu, and these qualities

[10] Page 27.

[11] Corre has also written a unique book on the criminality of the Creoles, *Le Crime en pays créoles* (1899), which I have not been able to obtain. An extract from this book may be found in the *Archives de l'anthropologie criminelle*, IV (1889), under the title: "Facteurs généraux de la criminalité dans les pays créoles."

[12] *Crime et suicide*, p. 129.

maintain themselves in spite of him. This is what forms the ethnic element." [13]

In the second work mentioned above, the author characterizes the connection between the temperament, race proper, and types of crime: "A race's temperament, the extent and form of its culture, impress a special quality on its activities, which one recognizes in its forms of crime. The African seems brutal and naïvely scheming to us; the Asiatic refined in his violences, cruel and astute; the European cynical, full of cold passion, often very reasonable during his worst misdeeds." [14]

The well-known German criminologist, Naecke, though very much taken in by the milieu-as-cause theory of crime, is convinced of the importance of race in its etiology. The races are neither physically nor spiritually equal in value.

If one believes in the dissimilarity of the principal races in physical and psychical respect, then, consequently, one must conclude that the physical and psychical abnormalities and deficiencies in conscience will show certain quantitative and qualitative variations. And this, indeed, seems to be the case, especially where crime and psychosis are concerned. Unfortunately the circumstances are so complicated that it is difficult to separate the real influence of race, and therefore one is restricted to a smaller or larger degree of probability.[15]

On the concrete treatment of the problem of race and crime Naecke goes no further. He bases his opinion rather on the great differences which races show in psychopathic point of view (insanity and suicide). The German people incline

---

[13] *Ibid.,* p. 130.
[14] Corre, *L'Ethnographie criminelle,* p. 23.
[15] "Rasse und Verbrechen," *Archiv für Kriminal-Anthropologie und Kriminalistik,* XXV (1906), 64.

more to melancholy (much suicide) and the Slavic and Romance peoples to mania.

In National Socialist Germany, where race is exalted to being the *deus ex machina* of community life, a great interest for the anthropological school naturally exists also among criminologists. One could call it "neo-Lombrosian." [16] One of the forerunners is Ploetz, an anthropologist of repute, the founder and director of the *Archiv für Rassen- und Gesellschafts-Biologie,* but now one of the worst zealots of the new theory.[17] Lenz, in his "Erblichkeit der geistigen Eigenschaften" (in Baur, Fischer, Lenz, *Menschliche Erblehre*), points out the great security of life and property enjoyed in North Europe. He asserts that this is to be ascribed to race. "Self-control, foresight, self-respect preserve the Nordic peoples to a great extent from breaking the law." [18] Not even the suggestion of proof is offered. Biologists like Lenz never suspect the existence of social influences. Results are reported in the first *Bericht der kriminalbiologischen Sammelstelle des Bayerischen Staates* (1926) of an investigation in the Institute directed by Viernstein at Straubing. They refer to 600 criminals who were examined concerning their race, among other things. The compiler asserts that the conclusions show race to be significant in the question of crime. However he still expresses himself cautiously, for which there is a good reason, since the composition of the race of the Bavarian

---

[16] The publication founded by Aschaffenburg in 1904 under the title *Monatsschrift für Kriminalpsychologie und Strafrechtsreform* has even had to change its title to *Monatsschrift für Kriminalbiologie und Strafrechtsreform!*

[17] See the section on Sozialanthropologie, in "Anthropologie," Deel III, afd. V, from *Die Kultur der Gegenwart.* It contains nothing remarkable or new.   [18] Page 743 (4th edition, 1936).

population is really unknown. Günther, for instance, judges the percentage of Nordics to be 50, while the Institute judges it to be 15.

In retrospect one might say that a sort of connection between races and a particular inclination to perpetrate certain offenses appears to exist in recognizable outlines. But it seems still more evident that races have, in general, a share in the total criminality which differs both relatively and positively. Only after long years of research on a material numerically much greater will the proof of the existence of these laws be rendered possible. For today one can again declare that when it is proved in general that a certain race maintains a high percentage of criminality, the explanation of this must be sought in a psychical constitution which is inherent in the race.[19]

In order to avoid all logical difficulties, the premise in the last sentence is made from the very thing which must be proved!

Under the Nazi regime, as we have said, criminal-anthropological thought has come to the fore. One of the most prominent of their men, Mezger, attacks the problem in his *Kriminal-politik* (1934) but gets nowhere with it.[20] No doubt he finds the question too thorny. Wagemann, also, in his article on the subject in the *Handwörterbuch der Kriminologie* (1936) is very cautious in his conclusions, and seems not to know what to do with the whole problem.[21] The only special study is, in my opinion, that of R. L. Martin, *Rasse und Verbrechen* (1937), an examination made of somewhat less than 300 Hessian prisoners; a rather superficial, uninformative little book. Although he is very much attracted by the race theory, the author concludes modestly:

[19] *Rassenkunde des deutschen Volkes,* p. 26.
[20] Pages 143–44.   [21] II, 454 ff.

We see, in general, all races in all types of crime. According to my observations of the Hessian criminals, I would deny that certain races are inclined to certain crimes. I can indeed say, however, that in my material the greater part of the Hessian criminals were of the Eastern race. That is to say, if my conclusions can be borne out in larger experiments, the Eastern type, in the reciprocal action of inheritance and environment, turns the more easily to crime, in the broadest sense of the word.

Naturally, however, the limitations of the material must again be considered, and therefore I believe that conclusions of general value have not yet been reached.[22]

The latest research on the connection in question is that of Exner, known, among other things, for his excellent work on *Krieg und Kriminalität in Oesterreich* (1927), and the director of the interesting *Kriminalistische Abhandlungen*. It is the latest, and, as I see it, the best publication coming from this group. Its point of departure, that the criminality of a people is also dependent on its character, is naturally indisputable. However he slips over the difficulty of judging how far the character is dependent on inherent (race) qualities. The most important part of the book is on Germany. He considers that the low rate of criminality in North Germany is to be attributed to the preponderance of Nordics there. However he expresses himself cautiously. "I should like to speak for the moment only of probabilities. These probabilities could be proved by sound research." [23] We shall return later to this scholarly work, when speaking of the criminality of the Nordic.

It appears on looking over the preceding statements (the

[22] Pages 36–37.
[23] "Volkscharakter und Verbrechen," *Monatsschrift für kriminalbiologie und Strafrechtsreform*, XXIX (1938), p. 421.

special studies on parts of the problem will be discussed later) that the discussion is not beyond its first stage—that of organizing the subject. There has been much asserted, but little or nothing proved. The strongest criticism to be made is that the question itself is barely defined theoretically, and is not at all clearly expressed. In the following section an attempt will be made to do these things.

THEORY

On reviewing the literature of criminology, we are struck by the slight theoretical consideration given in it to the nature of a possible connection between race and crime. The lack of material on this subject is due to the fact that too little account is taken of what "crime" really is. The impression is given that crime is a quality like the possession of blue eyes, a dark skin, musicality, and so forth. If this were so, then criminality would appear in all the individuals of a certain race, and in none of another race.

To express the problem in this way, however, is quite wrong. Criminality is not a characteristic. It is comparable neither to a physical quality such as the possession of blue eyes, nor to a spiritual one such as musicality. No one comes into the world with "criminality," in the way in which one is born with a certain color of eyes, and so forth. Crime is something completely different.

Elsewhere I have defined crime as follows: "Crime is a serious antisocial action to which the State reacts purposely through the application of a penance (punishment or other measure)." [24] In connection with this, one can define the

[24] *Inleiding tot de criminologie,* p. 7.

criminal as someone whose inclinations (generally vital) go against the interests of the community. At a certain moment these inclinations are stronger than the restraints (the normal ones, and those of self-interest). Consequently, criminality is the ascendency of the antisocial inclinations (generally vital) over the restraints.

Regarded from this angle, it is certainly great nonsense to speak of criminal and non-criminal races. Such things do not exist, and are not even to be imagined. Try to imagine all the members of a race as "born" thieves! The truth is, naturally, that crime occurs in all races, and, by the nature of things, is only committed by a number (generally very limited) of individuals in each race. In principle the races do not differ.

The problem in criminology is therefore quite different. It is this: Do the races differ quantitatively in their elementary inclinations? Though these inclinations in themselves have nothing to do with crime, still, *under certain circumstances* they can acquire an antisocial character. Thus the persons who have these inclinations in stronger degree than others are more predisposed to crime. And do the races differ in temperament, for instance in emotionalism? Not that temperament, in itself, has anything to do with crime, but again *under certain circumstances* it can increase the intensity of desire and therefore increase the urgency for its expression. And do the races also differ in the power and readiness of their restraints (moral restraints and those of self-interest)? By the nature of things, the answer can be of great, even decisive importance in our case. Indeed, the

differences in predisposition to crime among the individuals
of one race lie chiefly in this field.

These probable differences between the races are not absolute but are relative; the question is always one of *more*
or *less*. This has already been pointed out in my Introduction
and need not be repeated here. I also spoke of the great difficulties which are confronted in considering the question
of whether these differences are inherited or acquired. The
environment is, indeed, of great importance in the intensity
and the direction of the inclination. It is of even greater importance in the force and readiness of the restraints. (This
is one of the main objectives of education.) The temperament is certainly much less easy to influence, since it lies
more deeply rooted from a psychological point of view. It
is, however, certainly not altogether removed from the influences of milieu. This is especially true of the secondary
function which can be highly developed. The famous phlegm
of the English may be partly inherited, but for the greater
part it is inculcated in the home, at school, and on the sport
fields. Not until all the possible differences in milieu have
been eliminated do we come to the real question of the relationship between race and crime.

The difficulties which arise from the preceding points
are not inconsiderable. But they really begin to pile up
when one passes on to the treatment of the concrete problem:
Do the races differ in criminality? In order to answer this
question one must turn to criminal statistics, and these, one
finds, are very disappointing for that purpose.

Of the three great races, the Mongolian must at once be

counted out. China has not yet reached the level of social development in which such an institution as criminal statistics would exist. Although there are, thus, no exact data, there are still authors who express themselves on the criminality of the Chinese. Corre, for instance, in his *Crime et suicide* asserts that the Chinese "have little pity and a mediocre sense of honesty, are cruel to a refined degree, very deceitful. Their feelings spring from egotism . . ." [25] On the question as to how far these qualities are inherent he says: "To what degree have the Chinese an intrinsic tendency to crime? I could not say. I believe, however, that crime among them is more intensive than frequent." [26]

The criminality of the Chinese in the United States, especially in California, is of more scientific importance for the race problem because we have more or less accurate figures on it. It is not extensive. Furthermore, it is diminishing and is not of a serious nature. The authors who have occupied themselves with the problem find the explanation in social circumstances, and do not have recourse to the race hypothesis. To quote Hayner, for example:

The extent to which Orientals in America are incorporated in family groups, the closely related sex-age formation, the type of community influence, the contacts in America, and the distinctive cultural heritage are significant social factors for the explanation of variations in Oriental criminality. Generally speaking, criminality is low when a normal balance between the sexes makes possible a large amount of family life, and when

[25] Page 137.
[26] See also, by the same author, *L'Ethnographie criminelle*, chaps. v and vi. Also, L. Lorion, *Criminalité et médecine judiciaire en Cochin-Chine;* Matignon, *Superstition, crime et misère en Chine*, 4th ed.; and Fano, "Criminali e prostitute in Oriente," *Archivio di Psichiatria*, XV (1894).

a strong community organization maintains national traditions and prevents too rapid Americanization. . . . On the other hand, criminality is higher where there is an abnormal sex ratio, little family life, a weak community organization, and disorganized contacts with Americans.[27]

On the grounds of the facts which he has examined, Beach dismisses the race hypothesis: "Whatever one might expect to find, it is clear so far that there is nothing to indicate some special variety of crime which characterizes either the Chinese or the Japanese as racial stocks; nor is there any ground upon which to erect a theory of inborn racial tendency toward types of criminal behavior. . . ." [28]

In Japan criminal statistics have existed since 1875. A summary containing some of the most important data is given in the *Résumé statistique de l'Empire du Japon*, published yearly, in the French language, since 1887. It contains nothing which concerns our problem. It is not possible to make international comparisons with these figures. I have explained elsewhere the general objections to this sort of comparison.[29] Only in certain cases are they of some use; we shall come to this in speaking of Europe. It is completely impossible to make comparisons between Japan and European countries.

The Japanese population in the United States shows slight tendency to crime, even slighter than the Chinese. In this case, also, the authors above mentioned deny the significance

[27] "Social Factors in Oriental Crime," *American Journal of Sociology*, XLIII (1937–38), 919.
[28] *Oriental Crime in California*, p. 63. See also: Reynolds, "The Chinese Tongs," *American Journal of Sociology*, XL (1934–35), 612 ff.
[29] "Over criminele statistiek," *Tijdschrift voor Strafrecht*, XLVIII (1938), 452 ff.

of the race factor. The differences between the criminality of the Chinese and of the Japanese have just as little to do with race. ". . . these differences are all social-historical; they concern cultural contacts, and are evidently in no sense racial." [30]

We come now to the dark-skinned races. In the Philippines criminal statistics are recorded. The only study I know of on this subject considers that race is not a significant factor.[31] Filipino criminality in the United States is not slight, but it is diminishing. Hayner, in his above-mentioned study, points to the social factors in this phenomenon.[32]

In Indonesia criminal statistics have been recorded since 1907. Their publication, however, was abandoned in 1931. They give a rough division between the delinquents as follows: Europeans, foreign Orientals (Chinese, etc.), and natives. In the statistics for 1930 one can find the relative criminality of these groups (that is, per 100,000 of the population) computed as follows: Europeans, 12.34; foreign Orientals, 16.37; natives, 5.44. Considering the enormous differences in the social milieu of these groups, the figures are of no importance for the race problem.[33]

Aside from these studies there are also a few written by psychiatrists on the connection between race and crime. As van Loon remarks, psychopathology is also able to give information on the normal characteristics of races. "We have

[30] Beach, *op. cit.,* p. 95.
[31] Villamor, "Propensity to Crime," *Journal of the American Institute of Criminal Law and Criminology,* VI (1915–16).
[32] Pages 915 ff.
[33] In the *Indisch Militair Tijdschrift,* XLVII (1916), 867 ff., is an article by J. Meihuizen with statistics for the years 1913–15 on the criminality of the army according to races.

known for some time that general psychopathology presents us with the phenomena and the symptoms of ourselves in normal life, but in a 'macroscopic image,' much enlarged and much clearer; it could do the same for the different races." [34] Van Loon brings out, as an example, the fact that melancholia practically never appears among Malaysians, but mania appears very often.

In several publications, Dr. Amir has called attention to the criminality of various races as this is witnessed in the psychopathic department of the Glodok prison. Aggressive criminality there, for example, appears to be very slight among the Sudanese and Javanese (0.16 and 0.26 respectively, per 100,000 population) and very great among the Achinese and Buginese (1.80 for each). [35] The author himself calls attention to the fact that, for various reasons, no absolute value can be attached to his statistics, and he points out that "one would err in thinking that the emotional nature alone could cause an aggressive crime to be committed." [36] Milieu influences (prosperity, culture, and customs) are additional factors. It is interesting to note that all forms of psychopathy which appear in Europe are also found in Indonesia, and that the percentages of constitution-types (Kretschmer) for both groups (normal persons) are about the same. [37]

[34] *L'Organisation de l'étude comparative de la psychologie des races,* p. 90 (3d Session de l'Institut International d'Anthropologie, Amsterdam, 1927; Paris, 1928).

[35] "De inheemse psychopathen en hunne sociale beteekenis," *Koloniale Studiën,* XVII (1933), 443–44.

[36] "Over inheemse psychopathen en hunne forensische beteekenis," *Geneeskundig Tijdschrift voor Nederlands-Indië,* LXXIV (1934), 857.

[37] "Constitutietypen bij crimineelen," *Geneeskundig Tijdschrift voor Nederlands-Indië,* LXXIX (1939), 544.

Van Wulfften-Palthe points out that the real organic psychoses (dementia senilis, dementia paralytica and the schizophrenics) appear in practically equal numbers in Indonesia and in Europe, though this is not true of the lighter forms (neuroses, psychopathics and so-called reactive psychoses). These last, however, stand in close relation with the structure of the community.[38]

If the problem of the connection between race and crime in Indonesia is to be brought to a more definite solution, then we must know more than we do at present about the race psychology of the non-criminal population. These researches are now in their inception. Though Kohlbrugge wrote in his *Blikken in het Zieleleven van de Javanen en hunner overheerschers* in 1907 that he "was little interested in the so-called differences in race," [39] still this work, which rests on impressions more than on investigation, cannot hold up under serious criticism.[40]

Nieuwenhuis investigated the disposition of the Malaysians in regard to their imaginative faculties, and comes to the following conclusion: ". . . that in their industry the Malaysian peoples of the Indian Archipelago give evidence, where their imaginative powers and their individual development are concerned, of being able to compete with European peoples, but that nevertheless in this development the in-

[38] "Geestesstoring en gemeenschapsstructuur" (*Geneeskundig Tijdschrift voor Nederlands-Indië*, LXXVI, 1936. Overdruk p. 11). See also by this author, *Forensische psychiatrie in Nederlands-Indië* (Verslagen van het Psychiatrisch-Juridisch Gezelschap, No. 18, 1936).

[39] Page 125.

[40] See the crushing criticism by Snouck Hurgronje in *De Gids*, 1908, pp. 423 ff.

fluence of milieu makes itself strongly felt." [41] He comes to about the same conclusions where their faculty of memory is concerned.[42] In *De psychische eigenschappen der Maleische rassen,* van Loon (while admitting that knowledge of the subject is still limited) believes it is possible to conclude that the psyche of these races and that of Europeans differs quantitatively but not qualitatively. The Malaysian, he finds, is endowed with limited energy, a strong primary function, and an outspoken but otherwise controlled emotionality; the nervous type predominates, the psyche is primitive. During the discussion following his report, these hypotheses were strongly attacked.[43] They were later developed however, on the basis of experimental investigation by van Loon.[44]

All in all, one can hardly speak of a beginning of research in this field. There is no certainty that the qualities mentioned, if they are present, are inherent.

Von Mayr, in his *Statistik und Gesellschaftslehre,*[45] informs us on British India. Criminal as well as police statistics appear in that country under the title *Statistics of India.* From the data furnished by von Mayr it is not possible to discover whether account has been taken of the numerous races inhabiting India. I have been able to find nothing in

[41] Die Veranlagung der malaiischen Völker des Ost-Indischen Archipels, *International Archiv für Ethnographie,* XXI (1913), 54.

[42] *Ibid.,* XXII (1915), 191.

[43] Report of the Indisch Genootschap, meeting of Feb. 22, 1924, at The Hague.

[44] "Rassenpsychologische onderzoekingen," *Psychiatrische en Neurologische Bladen,* XXXII (1928), 190 ff. See also Travaglino, "De schizophrenie en de Javaansche psyche," *ibid.,* XXXI, 1927.

[45] III, pp. 514–16.

the literature known to me on crime in India which is of scientific interest on this point.[46]

Little, too, is known criminologically of the races living on the east and south shores of the Mediterranean. Barge calls them the Orientalitic and the Transmediterranean races.[47] Ammoun, in his book on Syria, does not mention race as a factor in crime, but explains the existing criminality there from social causes.[48] In his study on Egypt, El Kolaly does mention race as a factor, though it appears that he ascribes both the character of the Fellahs (the original population of the land) and that of the Arabs to their position in the community—small tenant farmers against nomads. The vendetta is a phenomenon appearing in all races at a certain stage in their development.[49]

We are somewhat better informed, from a criminological viewpoint, on the French colonies in North Africa, although in substance these studies are in the department of legal medicine. Several pupils of Lacassagne, head of the French school, have devoted their attention to it. Kocher, in his *De la criminalité chez les Arabes* (1884), is first on the list. He describes the native population, very mixed, as "quick and excitable," [50] inclined to deeds of violence, mostly the result of jealousy and vengeance. He hesitates to ascribe this to the race and explains their conduct rather by their manner of living (Nomadic tribes). In his study on Tunis,

[46] Corre, *L'Ethnographie criminelle*, chap. iv; Morrison, *Crime and Its Cause;* H. L. Adam, *Oriental Crime* and *The Indian Criminal;* E. C. Cox, *Police and Crime in India;* S. M. Edwardes, *Crime in India;* B. S. Haikerwal, *Economic and Social Aspects of Crime in India.*
[47] *De rassen der menschheid*, pp. 33–35.
[48] *La Syrie criminelle.*
[49] *Essai sur les causes de la criminalité actuelle en Egypte*, pp. 158 ff.
[50] Page 13.

Bertholon calls attention to the strong resemblance between the criminality of the Berbers and that of the population of the large Mediterranean islands and of the south of France. He mentions race in this connection as well as important social factors.[51] According to Arène's book on the Arabs in Tunis, most of their crimes are of a passionate nature, or spring from feelings of rivalry and vengeance. He does not mention race factors. The vendetta, he finds, is practiced by all races.[52] Arrii calls the Algerians suggestible and coarse. According to him they are not emotional, though they are easily led to crimes of passion. Their nature is to be explained partly by their manner of living ("very bizarre customs, habits, religion and superstitions").[53] He goes no further with the problem of race influences.

We have some information on criminality among the Negroes of South Africa. The South African criminologists Willemse and Rademeyer give some figures from prison statistics in which it appears that the criminality of the Negroes and of the British Indians is much greater there than that of the whites. Of 100,000 whites there was an average of 63.7 in prison, according to the figures compiled each December 31 for the years 1928 through 1931. At the same time there was an average of 248.2 Negroes, and 391.5 British Indians in prison.[54] In considering these figures, one must take into account the fact that the whites, for numerous

[51] "Esquisse de l'anthropologie criminelle des Tunisiens muselmans," *Archives d'Anthropologie Criminelle,* IV (1889).

[52] *De la criminalité des Arabes au point de vue de la pratique médico-judiciaire.*

[53] *De l'impulsivité criminelle chez l'indigène Algérien,* p. 38. For material on these races, see also Corre, *Crime et suicide,* pp. 140 ff. and *L'Ethnographie criminelle,* chap. ii.

[54] *Kriminologie,* p. 106.

reasons (better legal defense, etc.) are less frequently sentenced than the others. The greater criminality of both last-mentioned groups, as well as the nature of their crimes, is connected with their greater impulsivity and limited mental development. The authors do not go further with the question as to how far these qualities are inherent, racial characteristics.

We are quite well informed, both sociologically and psychologically, on the criminality of the Negroes in the United States. In a study on the connection between race and crime, this criminality forms the *pièce de résistance*. We will treat it in detail in the following chapter.

Finally we come to the white population of Europe. Most of the European countries have criminal statistics.[55] However, the population of each country is made up of several races, and on this point no direct data are given in the statistics. Where there is a great racial mixture, the correct filling in of census cards would be very difficult.

From one point of view, the statistics on the church membership of those convicted comes to our aid, for example, in the case of the Jews, where religion and race coincide. According to specialists in this branch, the Jews do not form a race,[56] certainly not a *single* race (Sephardim and Ashkenazim), though from an anthropological point of view they form a somewhat separate group. Jewish criminality, therefore, forms the second subject of our discussion.

Finally, the various races within a single country gener-

---

[55] See my previously mentioned study on criminal statistics, pp. 419 ff.

[56] Ripley says: "The Jews are not a race, but only a people" (*The Races of Europe*, p. 400), and Pittard: "il n'y a pas . . . de race juive" (*Les Races et l'histoire*, p. 430).

ally inhabit various sections of it. Thus the geography of crime can be of use to us, even if in an indirect and approximate way. International statistics also, where they show great difference in national tendencies to crime, may, when used with reservations, be of some significance.[57]

As we have said above, the races are very mixed—for example, the Alpines and the Nordics. Also we have yet to consider those racial mixtures in which the races are anthropologically the farthest apart, for example that of the whites and Negroes in North America, and of whites and Indians in South and Central America. Here are a few remarks on this hybridity before we turn to the detailed studies.

This subject, so far as I know, was first mentioned by Clémence Royer at the Second International Criminological Anthropological Congress at Paris in 1889, during a discussion of the "latest researches in criminal anthropology." She asserted that half-breeds are sometimes gifted in vitality and intelligence, but have no consciences (!). As proof of this she believed she could point out the great periods of civilization in which the most immoral proceedings frequently occurred, and during which mixed marriages were numerous.[58]

Corre, in his *Ethnographie criminelle* (1894), recognizes the fact that there is not yet enough material available to solve this problem. He names some favorable and some unfavorable examples of mixed parentage.[59]

A study by Nina-Rodrigues, *Métissage, dégénérescence,*

---

[57] See Bonger, *Over criminele statistiek,* pp. 453–55.
[58] Discussion of "Les dernières recherches d'anthropologie criminelles" (*Actes du IIme Congrès International d'Anthropologie Criminelle,* 1890), p. 172.   [59] Pages 29–32.

et crime,[60] concerns Brazil (Bahia) as well as other South and Central American countries of very mixed population. The region (Sarrinha) examined by the author contains many degenerates, a condition which, according to him, is the result of racial mixture. His assertion is not convincing, for he recognizes that there is present much alcoholism, syphilis, and interbreeding. The criminality in this region is slight, but where it does appear it is the result of degeneration, which he finds originating in mixed marriages. The study does not make a convincing impression.[61]

Naecke, in his previously mentioned study, *Rasse und Verbrechen*, is inclined to attach some importance to race mixture. He finds, however, that one must also take into consideration the very difficult circumstances in which the half-breeds ordinarily live. Race mixture can produce favorable as well as unfavorable results. The more the two races differ from each other, the less favorable are the results of the union.

To conclude, Weinberg, in his *Psychische Degeneration, Kriminalität, und Rasse*,[62] has made some remarks on the problem in question as it is found in Russia. On the basis of figures from the Russian census of 1897 (prison statistics) which appear to indicate some difference between the criminality of the Russians, Poles, Letts, Lithuanians, and Jews, he believes he can ascribe some importance to the race fac-

[60] *Archives d'Anthropologie Criminelle*, XIV (1899), pp. 477 ff.
[61] I have no further information about South and Central America. The criminal statistics of the countries there are but slightly or not at all developed. I have been unable to make acquaintance with their literature, not being familiar with the Spanish language.
[62] *Monatsschrift für Kriminalpsychologie*, II (1906), 720 ff.

tor, especially in connection with the bad results of racial mixtures which principally affect the character.

When one consults the literature of anthropology, it appears that no agreement exists on the grounds of favorable or unfavorable results of race mixtures.[63] The admirers of a particular race, from Gobineau to Madison Grant and Günther, are naturally convinced that race mixture is wrong and at some future time will cause the downfall of the superior Nordic race, and with it the whole of civilization. Others, such as Boas, deny that anything is known about the unfavorable results of race mixture. Others again, among whom are Bouman and Kretschmer, ascribe a very favorable action to such mixtures (numerous cases of genius and talent where the Nordics and Alpines have mixed). The question, thus, is apparently not ripe for solution. The general opinion does come to the fore that race mixture of quite different races is not favorable.[64] The problem becomes exceedingly complicated also through the fact, recognized by all unprejudiced observers, that mixed breeds often live in very difficult circumstances [65] and occupy an ambiguous position in society.

[63] A good survey is to be found in Hankins, *The Racial Basis of Civilization*, pp. 328 ff.

[64] See, for instance, Frets, "Het rassenvraagstuk" (*Socialistische Gids*, XIX, 1934, p. 533).

[65] See, for instance, Braconnier, *De Kindercriminaliteit in Nederlands-Indië*.

CHAPTER III

Race and Crime. Case Studies

NEGRO CRIMINALITY

IN THE United States criminal statistics have been recorded
since 1932.[1] They are still very elementary and incomplete, offering no data on the problem which occupies us;
therefore we must seek help from prison and police statistics.
At the time the census is taken a detailed examination is

TABLE I

| | PRISONERS AND YOUTHFUL DELINQUENTS: 1910 | | | |
| | Total per Jan. 1. | | Sentenced during 1910 | |
Race	Number	Per 100,000 pop.	Number	Per 100,000 pop.
Whites	93,841	114.8	382,052	467.4
Negroes	41,729	424.6	108,268	1,101.7
Other colored ...	902	218.6	3,614	876.0
Total	136,472	148.4	493,934	537.0

made of the criminals in prison at that moment and also of
those whose sentences began during the year. Table I is
taken from the Census of 1910.[2]

The criminality among Negroes as shown here is con-

[1] See my study, previously mentioned: *Over criminele statistiek*, pp.
434–35, 440–41.
[2] U.S. Bureau of the Census, *Prisoners and Juvenile Delinquents in the
United States, 1910.*

siderably higher than that of the whites. In his Introduction, the commentator has expressly warned against considering these figures as accurate. "It must always be borne in mind that the amount of crime actually punished in different classes or communities may not bear a fixed or unvarying ratio to the amount of crime committed." [3] Crimes committed by Negroes are more frequently prosecuted than those committed by whites. Negroes are less well able to defend themselves legally, they are less often in a position to secure a good lawyer, and they are more promptly sentenced to prison.

More recent data taken from the yearly prison statistics confirms this (see Table II). [4]

These figures leave no room for doubt: crime among the Negroes is significantly higher than among the whites. It is three or four times higher among the men, and four or five times higher among the women. To me, this appears to eliminate the idea that actual criminality among the Negroes is no greater than among whites—even if the above-mentioned causes make it appear greater than it is.

Table III gives information about the nature of the criminality. [5] It demonstrates that the very crimes frequent among

[3] *Ibid.*, p. 91. Nearly all the authors who have studied this problem call attention to this fact. See, for example, Sellin, "The Negro Criminal; a Statistical Note," *Annals of the American Academy of Political and Social Science*, CXXX (1928), 52 ff.; Haynes, *Criminology*, pp. 79 ff.; Gault, *Criminology*, pp. 203–5; S. M. Robison, "The Apparent Effects of the Factors of Race and Nationality on the Registration of Behavior as Delinquent in New York City in 1930," *Publications of the American Sociological Society*, XXVIII (1934), 37 ff.

[4] Taken from Von Hentig, "Die Kriminalität des Negers," *Schweizerische Zeitschrift für Strafrecht*, LII (1939), pp. 35–36.

[5] *Ibid.*, p. 37.

the Negroes are the serious ones in which the causes mentioned (for example, more frequent denunciation) certainly have the least influence.

The most recent data on the United States, dealing with the first three quarters of 1938, give, in general, a confirma-

TABLE II

TERMS BEGUN IN STATE AND FEDERAL PRISONS
(PER 100,000 POPULATION OF 15 YEARS
AND OVER)

Years	Men		Women	
	Whites	Negroes	Whites	Negroes
1929	113.4	385.1	6.5	30.7
1930	124.0	416.3	5.8	25.2
1931	136.2	478.8	5.8	26.7
1932	128.0	483.8	5.6	27.2
1933	117.0	447.0	? [a]	? [a]
1934	107.1	436.4	5.3	25.6
1935	113.4	473.5	5.4	28.9

[a] Lacking in the official statistics.

tion of the above. There were arrested, per 100,000 of population over the age of 15: 164 whites born out of the United States, 444 whites born in the United States, and 1,175 Negroes.[6]

In conclusion, it must be remarked that the criminality of Negroes in the Northern States is considerably higher than in the Southern States, actually three to one.[7]

[6] *Uniform Crime Reports for the United States and Its Possessions,* IX (1938), 3.
[7] See M. N. Work, "Negro Criminality in the South," *Annals of the American Academy of Political and Social Science,* XLIX (1913), 75.

Given the greater criminality of Negroes, we now come to the explanation of it. In the first place, we must consider the question as to whether Negroes and whites occupy different situations in the community; criminal sociology has

TABLE III

Crimes	SURVEY OF MEN IN PRISONS, PER 100,000 POPULATION: AVERAGE FOR THE YEARS 1926–34	
	Whites	*Negroes*
Manslaughter (both homicide and by negligence)	3.9	32.8
Felonious assault	2.7	28.9
Rape	3.1	6.2
Theft (including that of autos)	24.9	64.1
Burglary	20.5	76.1
Robbery	12.0	31.2

conclusively demonstrated the great importance of this factor in the etiology of crime.

The circumstances in which the Negroes live are very different from those of the whites, and are strongly conducive to crime. When they were freed from slavery after the Civil War (1861–65), the Negroes were left to their fate under the most difficult conditions. Unadjusted to their entirely new surroundings, despised and oppressed by the whites, ignorant and uncivilized, they were the pariahs of the United States. In spite of the greatest difficulties, they have worked themselves a little way up, but are still held back in every respect by the whites. In industrial life they belong to unskilled labor, their pay is the lowest; in periods of unemployment they are the first and hardest hit; they live in the slums of the great cities of the North; they are far behind the whites in civilization; the percentage of their illiteracy is ten times higher than that of the whites; alcoholism makes the most victims among them.

In order to demonstrate all this with figures and facts one would require a whole book at least the length of this study. A reference to the literature of the subject must suffice.[8] Among American criminologists there is practically a uniform opinion that the social situation of the Negroes offers the complete, or nearly complete explanation of their high criminality. I will limit myself to quotations from two authorities. Sutherland concludes as follows:

A general comparison of the negroes and whites is a comparison not only of races, but also of different economic and cultural groups. If a valid comparison is to be made, it would be necessary to compare negroes of a specified economic status with whites of the same economic status; or negroes of a certain educational and cultural status with whites of the same status. There is nothing in the previous discussion of the frequency of crimes of negroes that proves any racial, as contrasted with cultural, differences between whites and negroes.[9]

Root ends his consideration as follows:

The writer as a psychologist feels sure that few white men can appreciate at all the tremendous accumulated effect through-

---

[8] See the very informative work of Dowd, *The Negro in American Life*, with an extensive bibliography. There is also a separate bibliography on the whole Negro problem in all its aspects: M. N. Work, *A Bibliography of the Negro in Africa and America*. The author is himself a Negro.
[9] *Criminology*, p. 106.

out a life of our caste system. Debarred from this and that by a thousand social taboos, the lot of the negro is unparalleled in the experience of any other race.

The negro criminal then, is the victim of a vicious circle of social, biological and economic causes; lack of education, no trade training commensurate with the intelligence he has; a set of moral, social and leisure habits adjusted to a rural Southern community; a victim of caste, forced to live in discarded houses of the dominant race; restricted in employment and social opportunity, the negro is forced daily to feel inferiority and humiliation in a thousand ways. All this must be given consideration in judging his status in the criminal world.[10]

The influences of milieu on the Negroes in the United States are such that one has a priori no need to consider other factors. Those who still believe that the great differences in crime of the two races cannot find their explanation here exclusively, must consider that these differences can be even greater among groups from a single race. Table IV,[11] taken from German statistics, is instructive on this point. In the case of felonious assault, for example, the extremes are as 1:40, that is, four times further apart than in figures comparing whites and Negroes for the same crime.

The realization of this fact does not diminish the importance of considering what is known of the psychology of both races and the extent to which this plays a part in criminology.

[10] *A Psychological and Educational Survey of 1,916 Prisoners in the Western Penitentiary of Pennsylvania*, p. 217. See also Fernald, Hayes, and Dawley, *A Study of Women Delinquents in New York State*, as well as Von Hentig, "Die Kriminalität des Negers."

[11] Taken from Prinzing, "Soziale Faktoren der Kriminalität," *Zeitschrift für die gesammte Strafrechtswissenschaft*, XXII.

TABLE IV (GERMANY)

BASED ON 10,000 PERSONS OVER 12 YEARS OF AGE
SENTENCED IN THE YEARS 1894–96

Occupation	All Crimes	Aggravated Theft	Rape, etc.	Felonious Assault	Man-slaughter	Arson
I. Agriculture						
(a) Employers	75.1	0.2	0.21	14.1	0.02	0.08
(b) Workers	142.1	3.1	1.67	36.4	0.05	0.36
II. Manufacturing						
(a) Employers	129.9	0.5	1.20	17.5	0.02	0.09
(b) Workers	234.5	5.8	2.98	57.5	0.06	0.19
III. Commerce and Transport						
(a) Employers	275.5	0.7	1.35	21.8	0.04	0.10
(b) Workers	222.6	6.7	2.22	26.3	0.05	0.06
IV. Domestics	52.8	2.0	0.06	1.4	0.01	0.12
V. Public Services and Liberal Professions	79.3	1.2	1.69	6.6	0.01	0.02
VI. Population over 12 years old	120.1	2.5	1.17	22.3	0.03	0.13

Lombroso gives the following vivid portrait of the North American Negro:

The principal thing is always . . . the stifling of the primitive, wild instincts. Even if he (the Negro) is dressed in the European way and has accepted the customs of modern culture, all too often there remains in him the lack of respect for the life of his fellow men, the disregard for life which all wild people have in common. To them, a murder appears as an ordinary occurrence, even a glorious occurrence when it is inspired by feelings of vengeance. This mentality is furthered in the Negro by his scorn of his white fellow-citizens, and by bestial sexual impulses.[12]

As is usually the case in Lombroso's work, nothing but assertions are offered, and these rest, moreover, on a gross ethnological blunder.

Fouillée asserts that the dominant characteristics of the Negro are:

Sensuality, a tendency to servile imitation, lack of initiative, horror of solitude, instability, inordinate love of singing and dancing, and unconquerable taste for glitter and ornament. He is a person of pleasure, light, gossipy, improvident, lazy.[13]

One could easily add to citations of a similar nature on the unfavorable characteristics of the Negro. On the other hand, one can cite many which point to a favorable character. "The Negro is . . . sensitive to praise, and even more sensitive to blame," says Von Hentig.[14] "The Negro also manifests a juvenile characteristic in his natural frankness and truthfulness." [15] His kindliness, friendliness, and good humor are praised by many.

If one would express the general impression of those who know the North American Negro, then one would say: He is childlike. He does not look very far ahead, he is not very accurate, he is fond of bright colors and finery, is easily distracted. These characteristics may, naturally, be inherent, but this is not necessarily so. Those who are familiar with ethnological literature know that these characteristics ap-

[12] *Neue Verbrecher-Studien*, p. 15.
[13] *Tempérament et caractère*, p. 327.
[14] "Die Kriminalität des Negers," p. 55.   [15] *Ibid.*, p. 403.

pear ordinarily in primitive peoples of all races. And it is not difficult to conclude that the distant ancestors of those who so scorn the Negroes once had these same characteristics.

A strong sensuality is a quality which, according to many, may be ascribed to Negroes.[16] If we accept this observation as accurate, it is still no proof that sensuality is a race characteristic.[17] In the eyes of civilized inhabitants of temperate climates, primitive and uncivilized people, especially when they live in warm zones, are considered to be decidedly sensual. Moreover the Negroes, when they were slaves, lived in unfavorable sexual circumstances. The solution of the problem of the extent to which psychical qualities are inherent can be better approached through experimental research.

These experiments, being, as we know, full of difficulties, offer but little solid material. In their summaries both Garth [18] and Viteles [19] come to the conclusion that the results are insignificant where temperament is concerned. Klineberg esteems that on the whole nothing has been proved.[20]

We come to more solid ground when we turn to the experimental intelligence test. Here are quite a number of tests, of which the most important are those of the United States Army (so-called Army tests). According to these, the level of intelligence of the Negro is roughly 25 percent lower than that of the whites. In the case of the so-called

[16] Nearly all authors agree that the Negroes are musical. This quality is certainly inherent to a large degree, though the fact has no importance for criminology.

[17] On the similarity of the races in sexual matters, see Hirschfeld, *Geschlechtskunde*, II, 636 ff.

[18] *Race Psychology*, p. 175.

[19] "The Mental Status of the Negro," *Annals of the American Academy of Political and Social Science*, CXL (1928), 173.

[20] *Race Differences*, p. 207.

Beta tests (non-verbal) the difference is even less; this is also the case concerning the Negroes living in the North. The results obtained by these Northern Negroes are even higher than those of whites living in the South.[21]

Considering the very different milieu influences of Negroes and whites, one still gets the impression—although without complete certainty—that the inherent intelligence of the Negro is less than that of the white man. Serious, unprejudiced writers such as Hankins,[22] Dowd,[23] Viteles,[24] Garth,[25] and Peters,[26] come to this conclusion. Dowd, Viteles, and Garth at the same time make reservations. Klineberg denies the difference.

As we have already said in the Introduction, however, the inherent intelligence is of little or no importance in the chances of becoming a criminal.

JEWISH CRIMINALITY

The criminal statistics of certain countries furnish us with information on Jewish crime; from them we take the data in Table V. It should be remarked that actually Jewish crime is proportionately less than these figures would indicate, since the Jewish group as a whole contains a higher percentage of persons of the ages 18–50 (the age group most given to crime) than does the rest of the population. The first statistics concern Germany.

---

[21] See J. M. Reinhardt, "The Negro: Is He a Biological Inferior?" *American Journal of Sociology*, XXXIII (1927–28), 256. On the subject of the intelligence of -criminal Negroes, see Murchison, *Criminal Intelligence*, pp. 201 ff.

[22] *The Racial Basis of Civilization*, pp. 318 ff.

[23] *Op. cit.*, pp. 390 ff.   [24] *Op. cit.*, pp. 166 ff.

[25] *Op. cit.*, pp. 43–45.   [26] *Rassenpsychologie*, chaps. viii and ix.

As far as economic crimes are concerned, the figures for the Jews are favorable in general, though they are unfavorable in the case of crimes committed by intellectual means (fraud). The Jewish record for sexual and aggressive crimes is also favorable, except for the insignificant misdemeanor, insult.

Table V (Germany) [27]

| | CONVICTED PER 100,000 OF POPULATION OLDER THAN 14, DURING THE YEARS: | | | |
| | 1882–1891 | | 1892–1901 | |
Crimes	Jews	All Others	Jews	All Others
Theft	81.7	255.8	80.0	230.8
Grand larceny	9.4	31.7	10.3	33.5
Receiving stolen goods	20.1	22.3	15.8	20.5
Fraud	90.7	44.2	113.0	61.2
Forgery	17.1	9.6	24.6	12.9
Rape, etc.	8.4	9.3	9.4	11.8
Malicious mischief	10.9	39.1	11.3	47.5
Insult	188.4	127.4	199.9	143.2
Felonious assault	54.0	161.5	75.3	231.5
Rebellion against authority .	15.0	39.1	13.3	44.0

Table VI covers a later period; as far as I know the figures for 1916 were the last which appeared. The general impression for this period is about the same as that for the preceding. We come now to the data on Austria (see Table VII). Here, also, the picture is much the same as in Germany. If one examines Jewish criminality in the various parts of

[27] From von Mayr, *Statistik und Gesellschaftslehre*, III, p. 829.

Austria (for lack of space we are unable to give figures on this), one finds that in the east (Galicia) this is of a primitive, rough character (theft, assault, and so forth). In conclusion, it is to be remarked that the criminality of Jewish young people and women is negligible.

In Table VIII (for Hungary), the results are about the same, the so-called commercial misdemeanors giving unfavorable, the other crimes favorable, figures.

A recent work by the Genevan statistician Hersch makes

TABLE VI (GERMANY) [28]

	CONVICTED PER 100,000 POPULATION IN THE YEARS:					
	1909–10		1915		1916	
Crimes	*Jews*	*All Others*	*Jews*	*All Others*	*Jews*	*All Others*
Theft	71.1	178.3	40.6	122.0	49.0	163.0
Embezzlement	47.8	45.3	23.5	25.4	19.0	24.0
Receiving stolen goods	14.5	14.0	9.5	13.0	15.6	18.0
Fraud	93.4	43.0	44.9	21.1	39.8	20.8
Forgery	27.4	11.1	10.3	6.6	10.3	8.4
Rape, etc.	4.4	8.2	3.7	4.7	2.9	3.6
Insult	130.2	92.2	53.8	39.5	51.7	35.5
Malicious mischief ...	5.6	30.4	3.0	14.6	2.1	13.9
Felonious assault	72.3	191.9	18.7	49.2	19.8	41.6
Murder, manslaughter	0.2	0.7	0.2	0.5	0.0	0.5

[28] From Segall, "Die Kriminalität der Juden in Deutschland während der Jahre 1915 und 1916 im Vergleich mit der Vorkriegzeit," *Zeitschrift für Demographie und Statistik der Juden*, N.F. I (1924), 40–41. I have seen mention of the two following publications on this subject, but have been unable to obtain copies of them: Böckle, *Der Juden Antheil am Verbrechen*, and B. Blau, *Die Kriminalität der deutschen Juden* (1906).

TABLE VII (AUSTRIA) [29]

	CONVICTED PER 10,000 OF POPULATION IN THE YEARS:	
	1885–1900	
Crimes	*Population as a Whole*	*Jews*
Theft	6.1	4.1
Fraud	1.1	3.8
Fraudulent bankruptcy	0.2	2.5
Usury	0.006	0.47
Felonious assault	2.1	0.4
Murder, manslaughter	0.19	0.07
Rebellion against authority	0.9	0.6

TABLE VIII (HUNGARY) [30]

	CONVICTED PER 100,000 POPULATION IN THE YEARS:			
	1904		1906–9	
Crimes	*Jews*	*All Others*	*Jews*	*All Others*
Theft	66.1	123.8	245.4	536.1
Receiving stolen goods ...	9.4	12.8	41.2	58.4
Fraud	11.0	2.7	49.4	14.5
Forgery	6.3	3.8	23.5	15.9
Fraudulent bankruptcy ...	12.9	0.5	64.9	1.6
Rape, etc.	1.7	2.9	1.7	7.0
Malicious mischief	3.0	6.0	5.9	27.8
Disturbance of domestic peace	1.7	4.9	6.3	20.7
Felonious assault	13.3	83.8	66.1	380.0
Murder	0.0	0.3	0.7	1.0
Manslaughter	0.0	1.3	0.7	5.2

[29] From Herz, *Verbrechen und Verbrechertum in Oesterreich*, p. 178. See also Herz, "Die Kriminalität der Juden in Oesterreich," *Archiv für Strafrecht*, LIV (1907). See also Hoegel, "Die Grenzen der Kriminal-statistik," *Statistische Monatshefte*, N.F. XII (1907).

[30] From J. Thon, "Die Kriminalität der Christen und Juden in Ungarn

it possible for us to present the following figures for Poland (see Table IX).

TABLE IX (POLAND) [31]

	CONVICTED PER 100,000 POPULATION IN THE YEARS 1924–25			
	IN FORMERLY RUSSIAN TERRITORY		IN FORMERLY AUSTRIAN TERRITORY	
Crimes	*Jews*	*All Others*	*Jews*	*All Others*
Petit larceny	63.3	215.8	86.4	687.7
Grand larceny	6.1	7.1	6.3	21.0
Robbery	0.97	3.76	0.07	1.64
Receiving stolen goods	18.6	16.9	22.0	27.4
Swindling	10.7	9.2	8.5	6.5
Rape	0.05	0.76	0.81	1.13
Felonious assault	0.19	2.81	3.4	32.8
Manslaughter	0.27	3.23	0.2	5.1
Infanticide	0.10	0.73	0.13	0.42
Forgery, etc.	7.0	4.5	1.2	1.3

The picture is once again about the same: generally very favorable for the Jews. It is again to be remarked that the criminality of Jewish women is exceptionally slight.[32]

---

im Jahre 1904," *Zeitschrift für Demographie und Statistik der Juden*, III (1907), 105, and H. Nathanson, "Die Kriminalität der Juden und Nicht-juden in Ungarn in den Jahren 1906–9," *ibid.*, VII (1911), 61. For the period 1924–28 one finds more recent data in Hacker, *Der Einfluss der Konfession auf die Kriminalität in Ungarn*, which in general confirm the above. The reader's attention is called to the very slight criminality of women.

[31] From *Le Juif délinquant*, pp. 38–39, 52, 57, 60, 65.

[32] The data at my disposal on Jewish criminality in Russia is not very important. See Kovalewsky, *La Psychologie criminelle*, p. 23; Ambrunn,

In conclusion, Tables X and XI give the figures for the Netherlands. In these tables it is not possible to make the comparison simply between Jew and non-Jew.

TABLE X (NETHERLANDS) [33]

	CONVICTED PER 100,000 POPULATION OLDER THAN 10 YEARS (YEARLY AVERAGE FOR THE YEARS 1901–9 CALCULATED PER 12–31–1904)				
Crimes	Protes- tant	Catholic	Israel- ite	No Church	Total Pop.
Theft	40.0	54.8	25.5	9.6	43.9
Aggravated theft	19.9	24.0	12.7	5.2	20.7
Receiving stolen goods	2.6	3.5	9.2	0.7	3.0
Embezzlement	8.6	9.3	13.1	1.9	8.7
Swindling	2.4	2.5	3.9	0.4	2.4
Offenses against public de- cency	1.9	3.4	2.0	0.5	2.4
Minor sexual offenses	1.2	1.0	0.3	0.2	1.0
Rape, etc.	1.5	2.2	1.5	0.7	1.8
Sexual offenses by school- teachers etc.	0.3	0.3	0.1	0.0	0.3
All sexual crimes	5.1	7.1	4.1	1.6	5.7
Rebellion against authority ..	25.9	37.0	13.2	12.2	29.0
Assault	74.4	98.2	43.2	20.1	80.1
Serious assault	8.5	11.0	3.9	1.9	9.1
Homicide and murder	0.4	0.6	0.5	0.1	0.5
All crimes	308.6	416.5	212.7	84.2	337.3

"Die Kriminalität der Juden in Russland," *Zeitschrift für Demographie und Statistik der Juden,* II (1906) and V (1909); and Goldberg, "Zur Kriminalität der Juden in Russland," *ibid.,* VIII (1912). The Finnish criminal-statistician Verkko, the most trustworthy guide in this, gives figures which indicate a minimal aggressive criminality (see Table XXIII).

[33] From Bonger, *Geloof en misdaad,* p. 10.

The data here are fairly well in accord with the previous figures. Only in the so-called commercial misdemeanors are the figures unfavorable to the Jews; the rest are favorable

TABLE XI (NETHERLANDS) [34]

	THE CONVICTED, BY CHURCH AFFILIATIONS, IN PERCENTAGES OF THE TOTAL CONVICTIONS IN THE YEARS 1910–15, AND 1919 TAKEN TOGETHER			
Crimes	Protestant	Catholic	Israelite	No Church
Theft	52.4	43.9	1.3	1.8
Aggravated theft	58.2	37.4	1.5	2.2
Embezzlement	56.3	37.8	2.5	2.6
Swindling	53.8	38.1	4.6	2.6
Receiving stolen goods	51.5	41.1	4.9	1.9
Offenses against public decency	48.7	46.9	1.9	1.7
Minor sexual offenses	72.6	24.1	1.4	1.7
Rape	59.7	39.0	0.0	0.0
Sexual offenses by schoolteachers	59.8	38.1	0.5	1.6
Rebellion against authority .	52.1	43.9	1.2	2.4
Disturbance of domestic peace	58.2	38.1	0.8	2.6
Assault	56.3	40.1	1.3	2.0
Serious assault	48.2	49.3	0.6	1.5
Manslaughter and murder ..	58.3	38.3	0.4	2.0
Population 20 years of age and over (Dec. 31, 1920)	54.4	35.0	1.8	7.3

to them. Table XII gives information on a more recent period in the Netherlands.

[34] From Feber, *De kriminaliteit der Katholieken in Nederland*, pp. 13–18.

Again the impression is favorable for the Jews, though it seems somewhat less so in this period than during the preceding period. If one takes into account the shifting of ages in groups, the impression becomes less unfavorable. Ordinary economic crimes (theft, etc.) have increased considerably, as well as sexual and aggressive ones.

TABLE XII (NETHERLANDS) [35]

Crimes	Protes-tant	Catho-lic	Israel-ite	No Church	Total
	CONVICTED PER 100,000 POPULATION, TEN YEARS OF AGE AND OLDER. AVERAGE FOR THE YEARS 1931–33				
All crimes	258.6	301.7	299.3	192.4	269.8
Theft	40.3	52.0	42.0	29.7	43.0
Aggravated theft	19.0	19.3	14.7	15.3	18.9
Receiving stolen goods . .	4.7	5.3	6.7	3.3	5.0
Embezzlement	10.0	11.0	20.7	7.7	10.3
Swindling	6.7	5.7	14.7	4.7	6.0
Offenses against public de-cency	7.3	9.7	9.0	5.3	8.3
Minor sexual offenses	1.0	0.47	0.67	0.47	1.0
Rape	5.9	7.4	7.3	3.1	6.17
Sexual offenses by teach-ers, etc.	1.8	1.8	0.3	1.1	1.4
Rebellion against authority	8.0	12.3	16.3	9.3	9.7
Assault	55.3	66.7	48.0	37.7	55.3
Aggravated assault	1.0	1.7	0.7	1.0	1.0
Manslaughter and murder	0.6	1.1	0.0	0.7	0.9

In concluding, attention is again called to the very slight criminality of Jewish young people and women.

[35] From Mok, "Godsdienst en misdadigheid," *Socialistische Gids,* XXIII (1938), p. 659.

When we come to a discussion of the reasons for Jewish criminality, we should begin by noting that in as far as these crimes are economic, they depend on economic factors. Where the Jews live in utter poverty, as in Galicia, they show an extensive poverty criminality. And when the economic crisis in the Netherlands struck them harder than other groups, their economic criminality increased more rapidly than did that of the others. About a century ago, when things were exceptionally bad for the Jews in Western Europe, quite a number of Jews were to be found even among the so-called gang criminals.[36] A number of proofs of this can easily be made.

Is the so divergent criminality of the Jews to be explained by their social milieu? Adhering to the opinion he expressed more than twenty-five years ago, the writer of this study still believes this to be the case.[37]

The Jews have a very special position in business life. They are hardly ever agriculturists; on the contrary, they are mostly found in commerce, especially in the small retail businesses, and in the professions. Wassermann has been of service in pointing out that the high figures for Jewish fraud,

---

[36] This may be the reason why so many traces of Yiddish are found in slang; Avé-Lallement has pointed this out in his *Das deutsche Gaunerthum* (1858). We must protest forcibly that in a recently published article by a certain von Leers, "Kriminalität des Judentums," scarcely anything except this historical circumstance was mentioned, while the fact that the present Jewish criminality is very slight was ignored. In order to give an example of the level to which German criminology has sunk, we need only mention that according to this author Karl Marx was actually trying to organize the underworld! A certain Mikorey, member of the Akademie für Deutsches Recht(!), has an article in the same volume of *Das Judentum in der Rechtswissenschaft* on "Das Judentum in der Kriminalpsychologie" which is a mixture of malevolence and nonsense. Such writers should be the objects of criminological studies rather than the authors of them.

[37] *Geloof en misdaad*, pp. 32 ff.

swindling, and so forth are those of occupational criminality.[38] One must not forget, also, that the Jews have been
occupied in commerce for many centuries, and have built
up a tradition of overwhelming importance. The superficial
"man in the street" says that the commercial spirit is "in
the Jewish blood," just as he says that the "peasant mentality," formed through the generations, is "in the blood."
But we must recall the fact that "peasant mentality," formed
through the generations, becomes lost again when country
people go to the city. The population of great cities consists
for the most part of the descendants of farmers. The Jews,
indeed, were once agrarian, and in Palestine they are today
becoming so again.[39]

In the second place, the Jews have been city dwellers for
centuries, mostly dwellers in great cities. They are even the
city dwellers *par excellence;* there is no race or subrace or
group of the population in the whole world which can be
compared to them in this respect.[40] Thus their criminality
has a city character,—that is to say, as far as economic crime
is concerned—it has an intellectual character. There are also
many Jews in the professions and their cultural level is gener-

---

[38] *Beruf, Konfession, und Verbrechen.*

[39] Although it is not within the scope of this study, the author here
permits himself a remark on anti-Semitism. One of the most important
factors, if not the most important factor in this, according to him, is the
fact that the Jews are mostly merchants from generation to generation.
The commercial spirit is hated by many: "Commercialism is the complete
system of egoism," says von Jehring in *Der Zweck im Recht.* It is naturally hated as much in non-Jews as in Jews, for it appears in non-Jews
to just as great a degree. On the other hand, there are many Jews—
scholars, artists—who have a completely different mentality and by whom
the commercial spirit is hated. No one has so lashed out against this commercial spirit as has the Jew Karl Marx.

[40] Kautsky has especially called attention to this. See his *Rasse und
Judentum.*

ally high. This partly explains the slightness of aggressive crime among them.

In the third place, the Jews form a minority wherever they are—mostly a small minority—and they are often victims of persecution. Their close unity, their mutual helpfulness, their family feeling are famous. Much care is given to the children (generally not numerous at present) in Jewish households. The criminality of youths among the Jews is generally slight.

In the fourth place, alcoholism is a comparatively slight factor among the Jews—this, in turn, for sociological reasons —and here again is a factor favorable to a low rate of aggressive crime.[41]

In conclusion, it must be remarked that in proportion as the Jews take a less isolated place in the community (mixed marriages, the whole process of assimilation) their criminality will more and more resemble that of the general mass of the population. Recent figures from the Netherlands show this in some degree.

The majority of writers agree with this opinion as I have stated it, e.g., Wassermann, von Liszt, Herz, Aschaffenburg, Hacker, Hersch. Some make certain reservations; they see the criminality of the Jews nearly, but not entirely, explained by these reasons. Others, again, such as de Roos and Sucrmondt,[42] although they see the social milieu as an important cause, believe that this, in turn, depends on racial factors. The former expresses it as follows:

[41] On this, see H. Hoppe, *Alkohol und Kriminalität*, pp. 122 ff., and "Die Kriminalität der Juden und der Alkohol," *Zeitschrift für Demographie und Statistik der Juden*, III (1907), and L. Cheinisse, "Die Rassenpathologie und der Alkoholismus bei der Juden," *ibid.*, VI (1910).

[42] "De criminaliteit onder de Joden," *Tijdschrift voor Strafrecht*, XXXIII (1923).

That the Jews turn by preference to commerce is not an accidental fact, but partly the result of the special intellectual disposition of the Jewish race. Thus, the evidence is not offered that the vocation factor is the *cause* of the Jewish share in certain misdemeanors, rather the choice of profession and these misdemeanors have a *common cause* in the characteristics of the Jewish people.[43]

This assertion brings us to the psychical race factor.

A stream of literature has appeared, on the inherent psyche of the Jews, which does not deserve to be classified as scientific. Expressions of antipathy, not based on research, certainly have no bearing on the question of whether the qualities mentioned are actually inherent. It is not important to mention these works. We will limit ourselves to a few of the most important authors who, whether one agrees with them or not, have followed a scientific method.

Sombart, in his *Die Juden und das Wirtschaftsleben* (1922) gives the following qualities as characteristic of the Jewish spirit: (1) intellectualism, that is, the placing of mental qualities above physical ones, and excelling in them; (2) rationalism, and a striving for the purposeful; (3) energy; (4) activity. Sombart has no definite opinion as to whether these qualities are inherent or acquired. Much of Sombart's work is susceptible to criticism (he has much overestimated the role played by the Jews in the origins of capitalism).[44] But his contention that the Jews, once a wilderness people, are so again because they live in the wilderness of great cities, though nothing more than a whimsy is still a striking char-

[43] "Ueber die Kriminalität der Juden," *Monatsschrift*, VI (1909–10), p. 206.

[44] In his zeal to demonstrate the greatness of the role of the Jews, Sombart has taken J. Pzn. Coen (Cohn!) for an example.

acterization, and many such are to be found in his work.

Steinmetz has expressed himself several times on the Jewish question, most recently in his *Sociologische rasproblemen,* which we have previously mentioned. After expressing sharp criticism of Sombart on many points, he arrives at the following factors in the Jewish spirit: sharp intellect, lively spirit, sense of practical reality, less emotionality (perhaps) and great energy.

Zollschan, in his *Das Rassenproblem* (2d edition, 1911), says: "The mental receptivity is incomparably greater in the Jews than in any other race anywhere, and therefore their perception is also cultivated to an extraordinary degree." [45] He considers the greater intelligence of the Jew— he gives examples from Vienna—to be a proven fact.

In his *Soziologie der Juden,* Ruppin describes the Jewish spirit as follows:

When we consider their intellectual talent, we may best call it invention, perception, organization, ambition in practical things, as well as intellectual liveliness or facility in grasping theoretical things, and rationalism in religious things. Probably all these qualities flow from the same source, from a capacity for quick association of ideas.[46]

He reports, in conclusion, a few investigations by means of the so-called intelligence tests, applied to school children. From these again appears the fact that has previously been established, namely that the Jewish are more "verbal," the non-Jewish more "real" in disposition.

Aschaffenburg considers that race is not a proven factor *in rebus criminologicis,* but he makes an exception of the misdemeanor of insult.

[45] Page 411.   [46] I, 53–54.

Though I thought that, in the case of the other defects, there was not enough evidence of the influence of racial quality, I believe that in [the misdemeanor of] insult there is an inner connection with race. The liveliness of character which manifests itself in gestures and play of features, in bombast and loud speech, in increased capacity for enthusiasm and irritability is much greater in the South than in the North.[47]

One of the few modern psychological works on the Jewish spirit appeared in the Netherlands, the *Bijdrage tot de Speciale Psychologie van het Joodsche Volk* by J. Leydesdorff (1919). It is based on an inquiry made by the author in which he frequently compares his results with those of the great research of Heymans and Wiersma. We call attention here to some of these results.

The mobility, as well as the activity and the impulsivity of the Jews is greater, the emotionality is quite considerably higher, than is the case with other races. Their intelligence stands at the top in a mixed group, their pride also. Greed for gold, dishonesty, but also generosity and helpfulness are strongly to the fore in Jewish character—also an inclination to exaggerate (extremism).

The classification of the Jews according to temperament shows a greater percentage of nervous, sentimental, and passionate types, and a lesser percentage of neutral and phlegmatic types. Nervous diseases, such as hysteria and neurasthenia, are more prevalent among the Jews than among the rest of the population.

In conclusion, it is worthy of note that certain authors, among others Forel [48] and Wulffen,[49] assert that the Jew

[47] *Das Verbrechen und seine Bekämpfung*, 3d ed., p. 61.
[48] *Die Sexuelle Frage*, p. 214.   [49] *Der Sexualverbrecher*, p. 302.

is more strongly sexual than is, for example, the Nordic. This is not proven (though early maturity is), but it can be considered quite possible; in what degree is not known.

On looking over the whole field,[50] one finds considerable agreement among Jewish and non-Jewish authors. Sharp (formal) intellect, emotionality, lively spirit, energy are more noted among Jews than among others; it is not possible to indicate to what degree. When one expresses these things in figures, as does Leydesdorff, the differences are not generally great. On the question of whether the differences are inherent, and thus belong to the race, the authors are not all in agreement. The majority, among whom is the writer of this study, believe them to be inherent. As to the extent of the inherent differences, opinions again differ sharply; as I see it, these opinions are often very exaggerated.

Of what significance can these psychical characteristics be in criminology? Some assert that the sharp intellect of the Jews is responsible for their greater share in such misdemeanors as fraud, and so forth, either directly or indirectly (through their choice of commercial employment, for example). This assertion, as I see it, is completely pointless. On the subject of intelligence as a factor in crime, the following is appropriate: *ni cet excès d'honneur ni cet indignité.* Intelligence is a weapon which can be directed for good or for evil. As far as the indirect connection goes, there is no point as I see it, in qualifying the Jewish intellect as a business intellect; the contrary would be more true. Their intellect is very suitable for commerce, but certainly no less

[50] A good review is also to be found in G. Schaaf, *Ueber die Besonderheiten des jüdischen Geistes und ihre Ursachen,* 1931.

so for science, in which field a disproportionately large part of the Netherlands Jewish population belong. I can see nothing of criminological significance in this factor, unless it is based on the naturally unproved theory that the Jews choose commerce as a calling in order to cheat. The truth is that the Jews, driven to it by the non-Jews, have been obliged especially to apply themselves to commerce.

As far as the other psychical characteristics are concerned, if the high emotionality (many nervous cases) does not correspond with the slight aggressive criminality, the lively spirit and the interest in things of the spirit, making for a high level of culture, does. The slight sexual criminality does not correspond to the assertion of high sensuality.

MEDITERRANEAN CRIMINALITY

As we have already stated, it is only in the cases of Negro and Jewish criminality that a direct approach is possible, at least for the present. The remaining races must be studied indirectly, though this method has many limitations. The races of Europe can be geographically located, though only in a very approximate manner, since they live side by side and there is much racial mixture. Thus, for example, when one says that central France is inhabited by the Alpines, one means to say that the Alpines form a majority there. A geographical determination of the criminality of this section of France has not proved but has only made possible an assumption of the extent of criminality in the Alpine race. In this way one could name many other difficulties. Only with many reserves will an attempt be made in the following sections to determine something about the criminality of the European races.

Since Ripley, three principal races [51] have been recognized in Europe: the Mediterranean, the Alpine and the Nordic. The anthropological characteristics of the first are: small frame; dolichocephalic skull; dark complexion, eyes, and hair. The Mediterraneans live chiefly around the western end of the Mediterranean sea, in Spain, south France, and south Italy.

What about the criminality of the Mediterraneans? The figures in Table XIII give some information on the subject. We limit ourselves here especially to aggressive criminality, with sexual criminality also mentioned; economic crimes, however, will not be considered. There is no reason, as I see it, to connect these latter with race, and to do so creates great statistical difficulties. Economic crime is caused either by poverty (in the strict meaning of the word) or by greed. Elsewhere [52] I have succeeded, I hope, in demonstrating that both phenomena are dependent on the structure of society, where one need call in no race theories. Crimes caused by misery have a connection, however, with the physical milieu, for instance, in warmer lands the minimum requirements of men are much less than in colder lands.

These figures show a very high aggressive criminality in

[51] A fourth division—the Dinaric race—was later recognized. This is a subdivision of the Alpine. Since, so far as I know, nothing is known about this race from a criminological point of view (their criminality is probably high, e.g., in the Balkans), it will not be further mentioned.

[52] See my *Criminalité et conditions économiques,* 1905 (American translation in 1915) and *Inleiding tot de criminologie,* 1932 (English translation in 1936).

TABLE XIII [53]

Countries	Years	Murder, Manslaughter, and Assault Where Death Results (Per Million Inhabitants)
Italy	1880–84	70.0
Spain	1883–84	64.9
Hungary	1876–80	56.2
Austria	1877–81	10.8
Belgium	1876–80	8.5
Ireland	1880–84	8.1
France	1880–84	6.4
Scotland	1880–84	4.4
England	1880–84	3.9
Germany	1882–84	3.4
Netherlands	1880–81	3.1

the lands where the Mediterranean peoples live, namely Italy and Spain. In Italy criminality of this type has sharply diminished and is no longer as bad as it formerly was. On Spain we have no recent data. But the figures are still unfavorable compared to those for the northern part of Europe—except for the Baltic States—as we see in Table XIV.

One need not weigh such international statistics on an assaying scale. There are doubts, especially in the last column; it is very doubtful, for example, whether Germany and Belgium are really so unfavorably placed. But nevertheless such contrasts as that of England, Netherlands, and the Scandinavian countries on the one side, and Italy and Spain on the other are certainly real.

[53] From Bonger, *Criminalité et conditions économiques*, p. 686.

TABLE XIV [54]

Countries		CONVICTED PER 100,000 OF ADULT POPULATION	
	Years	*Murder and Manslaughter*	*Assault*
Bulgaria	1929–30	22.3	1.5
Lithuania	1929–31	13.9	4.1
Latvia	1929–32	11.0	2.6
Esthonia	1927–28	10.0	9.0
Greece	1929–31	8.7	1.1
Poland	1932	7.3	?
Portugal	1929–32	5.6	?
Finland	1929–31	5.1	1.2
Hungary	1928–31	4.1	5.3
Roumania	1929–32	3.9	9.1
Italy	1926–27	3.8	3.3
Austria	1929–32	2.0	?
France	1925–28	1.6	1.2
Czechoslovakia	1929–31	1.4	2.2
Germany	1929–31	0.9	10.5
Switzerland	1927–32	0.9	1.2
Ireland	1929–31	0.8	0.1
Belgium	1928–31	0.7	6.8
Netherlands	1929–31	0.5	0.8
Denmark	1929–32	0.3	0.4
Sweden	1929–31	0.3	0.2
Norway	1929–32	0.2	0.5
England and Wales	1927–31	0.2	0.1

Consequently, aggressive criminality is great in Italy. The figure given, however, is the average taken from very di-

[54] From Hacker, "Statistique comparée de la criminalité," *Revue Internationale de Droit Pénal,* XIII (1936).

vergent figures for the different regions in Italy. The Sicilian and south Italian regions, where the Mediterraneans mostly live, present figures for the years 1880–83 of about 30 per 100,000 of population as against 2 per 100,000 in the north Italian districts.[55] In recent years aggressive crime has diminished greatly, but the comparison between north and south has remained unfavorable to the latter.[56]

The same situation existed in south France and Corsica in the first half of the nineteenth century. Quetelet has already called attention to the fact that one finds the maximum of aggressive criminality there,[57] and more recent times have proved this. Bournet, in his *De la Criminalité en France et en Italie* (1884) [58] and Guégo in his *Contribution à l'étude statistique sur la criminalité en France de 1826 à 1900* [59] both observe that in the case of manslaughter it is Corsica, Alpes-Maritimes, Bouches-du-Rhone—where the Mediterraneans especially live—which show the most.

Aggressive and sexual criminality is also great among the Italians in the United States. According to the Census of 1910, the figures for Italians accused of murder, manslaughter, criminal assault, and rape, per 100,000, are respectively 2.3; 8.0; 67.2; and 5.9. At the same time, figures for immigrants from a very favorably placed land like Denmark are respectively 0.0; 1.1; 11.6; and 0.6, while for the population in general they read 0.8; 2.2; 35.5; and 2.0.[60] Recent data for the years 1930–33 confirm these results. The criminality

[55] See my *Criminalité et conditions économiques*, p. 689.
[56] See figures by Roesner in *Handwörterbuch der Kriminologie* I, p. 690.
[57] See *Physique sociale*, II, p. 280.
[58] Page 40.   [59] Pages 32–33.
[60] U.S. Bureau of the Census, *Prisoners and Juvenile Delinquents in the United States*, 1910, p. 131.

of the Spanish far exceeds that of the Italians, and heads the list.[61]

The Italian immigrants in the United States, in a large majority of cases, come from the south of Italy. It has been proved through some special studies that the majority of Italian criminals in the United States is composed of southern Italians.[62] One can thus rightfully say that in America, also, the Mediterraneans are guilty of committing many crimes.

These are the facts, now come the explanations. For Lombroso, as usual, these do not offer any difficulties; that *deus ex machina*, race, explains everything. He seldom, if ever, mentions social conditions—even the Corsican vendetta, which has nothing to do with race, is not mentioned.[63] It may well be remarked here, parenthetically, that the Corsicans, when on the mainland of France, are not at all criminally inclined; on the contrary, there they have always been, and are today, respected members of society.

There is thus every good reason to connect the social milieu in which the Mediterraneans live with their criminality. They live, namely, in very different circumstances from the northern European. Spain and south Italy ("Italia barbara") were, and still are, semifeudal lands, where quite diffent conceptions of aggressive crime are prevalent.

Colajanni has described these conditions in a fine study, "L'Homicide en Italie." [64] Giardini has also done so in a

---

[61] See D. R. Taft, "Nationality and Crime," *American Sociological Review*, I (1936), 732.

[62] See, for instance, K. Claghorn, "Crime and Immigration," *Journal of Criminal Law and Criminology*, VIII (1917-18), 677, and G. Giardini, "A Report on the Italian Convict," pp. 219 ff. (in Root, *A Psychological and Educational Survey*).

[63] See *Le Crime*, pp. 31 ff.   [64] *Revue Socialiste*, XVII (1901), 34 ff.

recent study, where, having described the poverty in which the population of south Italy lives, he continues as follows:

To this status of affairs must be added the residual traditions inherited from the feudalistic system which prevailed throughout Italy, in fact all of Europe, during the last century, and is by no means extinct. This system—combined with a certain amount of neglect on the part of the Italian government—is responsible not only for some of the present economic conditions of this section of Italy, but for certain traditions,—found less often in the north, that are directly conducive to crime. Family quarrels, for example, are still very common, and are often perpetuated from generation to generation, as in olden days. The head of each family makes his own laws, in conflict, if necessary, with the laws of the State. As a result, the people tend to retain the habit of carrying weapons whenever they can, and abide by the biblical dictum of an eye for an eye and a tooth for a tooth. They are jealous of their possessions, be these chattels, spouse or honor, however this may be conceived. They are slow to forgive and seldom forget an injury.[65]

The author of the present study has himself demonstrated that aggressive crime, and also, to a certain extent, sexual crime, follow an international and national parallel with the cultural level of the great mass of the population.[66] The spiritual state of the primitive man is such that he is quickly led to thoughts of vengeance. This state leads to impulsiveness and keeps alive from still earlier times such conceptions as that of each individual's avenging himself. It is not conducive to leading the human spirit into other conditions which would encourage restraint from aggressive acts.

[65] Giardini, *op. cit.*, p. 223.
[66] See Bonger, *Criminalité et conditions économiques*, pp. 685 ff., and pp. 671 ff.

There is no more convincing proof that the social milieu, and not race, is the decisive factor than that offered by the great change in aggressive criminality in the whole civilized world in the latest period of history. Thanks to the material and spiritual improvement of the masses, aggressive crime has diminished, even in Italy.

In the United States, Italians of the second generation lose their aggressive nature and show about the same rate of criminality as the American born.[67] Sutherland produces the following table as proof of the rapidity of adjustment; in this connection one must not forget that the American milieu is far from free of criminal factors.[68]

TABLE XV

Nativity and Parentage	Commitments to state prison and state reformatory in Massachusetts for murder, manslaughter, criminal assault in the years: 1914–22 (Per 100,000 of Population)
Italy	192
America; one or both parents born in Italy	24
America; both parents born in America	24
America; one or both parents born in other countries	22

In his *Race Differences* Klineberg sums up his point of view on "aggressiveness" as follows:

Conflict may be inevitable, but culture determines its mode of expression. Whether an individual fights with satire or with

[67] Giardini, *op. cit.*, pp. 226 ff.   [68] *Criminology*, p. 102.

property or with his fists will be decided by the traditions and customs of his group. A form of behavior which makes him a hero in one society will bring him ridicule in another. There will still be differences between individuals, but the broad lines of behavior will be determined by the group. The "hot-headed" Sicilian and the "phlegmatic" Englishman are in all probability cultural products.[69]

The foregoing arguments do not prove, however, that race has no importance in the problem of crime. And this brings us to the psychological study of the Mediterranean. What we have quoted until now was not very deep and was based more on impressions than on scientific research.

In his *Rassenkunde des deutschen Volkes*, Günther gives these characteristics of the Mediterraneans (he calls them "Westische Rasse"); passionateness and liveliness of spirit.[70]

Fischer's characterization is the following:

From the mental point of view, the North and Central European is struck by the vivacity and instability of the Mediterranean race. A certain savageness and cruelty is theirs; little foresight, great capacity to imitate and let themselves be influenced. The intelligence is not high, and the fantasy not at all so developed as with the Nordics, the musical talent considerably higher.[71]

Kretschmer says in *Geniale Menschen* (1929) that "The impulse to cruelty and rashness, wild bursts of passion, is a common stigma of all Mediterraneans and mixed Mediterranean peoples." [72]

If we were to place the above, with all its implications, under the psychological microscope, there would probably

[69] Page 268.   [70] Page 178, 11th edition.
[71] "Specielle Anthropologie: Rassenlehre," in *Anthropologie*, p. 151.
[72] Page 85.

be a great deal to comment on. The "Nordic" expressions of Fischer especially would certainly not go uncontradicted. It is hardly admissible, for instance, that the Nordics are more intelligent and imaginative than the Mediterraneans. This, however, is of no significance in a criminological study. The only point of interest here is that concerning temperament and sensuality. On both points there is general agreement: the Mediterranean is of a violent temperament, he reacts quickly and vehemently and is of a sensual nature—to what extent no one knows, except roughly.

Many authors have named both these characteristics as factors in crime. Erroneously, as I see it, for in this way one can say that *all* human qualities are conducive to crime. One has equally little right, it seems to me, to call age a factor in crime, though the predisposition to crime varies greatly in the different age groups. The human desires are simply not of the same intensity in a person in the full flower of life as they are in a graybeard. Human desires can work for good as well as for bad ends—that depends, naturally, on countless circumstances. Under conditions conducive to crime they work toward the evil; under favorable circumstances, toward the good.

Just as this holds true for the individuals of a single race, so it is also true for the race taken as a whole. If a certain race, for example, contains a greater number of types of a violent temperament than another, then, under circumstances equally conducive to crime, it will show a greater number of aggressive criminals than the second. The decisive factor is, and remains, the criminological circumstances. Lacking these, a predisposition to violence is of no importance.

ALPINE CRIMINALITY

The second of the principal races of Europe is the Alpine. Its most important anthropological characteristics are: medium stature, brachycephalic skull, dark (brown) hair and complexion, tendency to corpulency. The Alpines, as their name indicates, inhabit the mountainous section of Central Europe, namely: central France (Auvergne) the western Alps (Tyrol and Switzerland) and southwest Germany. Naturally, one finds other races and mixtures in these countries, as well as Alpine elements in other places—for instance in southern Belgium (Wallonia) and in the southern provinces of Holland.

It is very difficult to determine the criminality of the Alpine population. There are few, if any, direct data on the subject.[73] There are no criminal statistics which mention the Alpine race. Thus we are forced to turn to the geography of crime, with all the drawbacks attending this method. When for instance, a certain section has a high rate of crime, and contains a quite high percentage of a certain race, then there is only a probability, but no certainty, that the criminals belong principally to that race.

Concerning France, it may be observed that the departments in the center take a middle position as far as their aggressive and sexual crime is concerned.[74] The same sort of crime in Belgium is less prevalent in the southern part than

[73] A beginning has been made with this problem, in the Beierse Kriminaal-Biologische Dienst, but it has not yet led to any very positive results. See *Statistisches Material der kriminalbiologischen Sammelstelle des Bayerischen Staates*, Bericht I.

[74] Bournet, *De la Criminalité en France et en Italie*, pp. 41 and 67.

in Flanders, where, actually, the Nordic element is stronger.[75]

In the Netherlands the matter is again different. Table XVI shows a comparison of aggressive and sexual criminality in the provinces of Holland. In Limburg, North Brabant, and Zeeland, the Alpine race is more prevalent (40 percent at most) in so far as we can determine it by stature [76] and coloring.[77] In the other provinces the Nordic race is more prevalent.

TABLE XVI (NETHERLANDS) [78]

Provinces	Murder, Manslaughter and Assault Where Death Resulted	Assault	Sexual Crimes
Limburg	5.8	126.8	3.5
North Brabant	3.1	98.3	3.1
Drenthe	2.9	171.6	2.4
Groningen	1.7	113.0	3.2
Overijssel	1.7	71.5	2.3
Utrecht	1.7	55.2	2.6
The Kingdom	1.7	66.2	2.4
North Holland	1.2	33.5	2.2
Gelderland	1.1	69.5	2.4
South Holland	1.1	35.5	1.5
Zeeland	0.7	77.9	2.6
Friesland	0.6	65.0	3.2

[75] Jacquart, *La Criminalité belge, 1868–1909*, p. 130.

[76] See Van den Broek, "De anthropologische samenstelling der bevolking van Nederland," *Mensch en Maatschappij*, VI (1930).

[77] Bolk, "De bevolking van Nederland in hare anthropologische samenstelling," in Gallée, *Het Boerenhuis in Nederland en zijn Bewoners.*

[78] From Bonger, "Misdaad en socialisme," *Nieuwe Tijd*, XVI (1911), 717 and 719.

These figures thus give but slight corroboration to the assertion that the Alpine race shows a high rate of criminality. Certairily Limburg and North Brabant present an unfavorable picture, but Zeeland is at the bottom of the list; Drenthe and Groningen also are unfavorably placed.

More recent data give another picture in Table XVII.

TABLE XVII (NETHERLANDS) [79]

Provinces	Manslaughter and Murder, Assault Where Death Resulted	Assault	Sexual Crimes
Limburg	3.0	75.4	13.4
Drenthe	3.0	68.7	4.9
Groningen	2.6	42.8	9.4
North Brabant	2.0	43.7	7.6
The Kingdom	1.5	40.9	8.4
South Holland	1.4	31.4	8.5
Friesland	1.3	31.6	8.9
Gelderland	1.2	40.4	7.2
North Holland	1.1	31.4	8.6
Utrecht	1.1	44.9	9.5
Overijssel	1.1	45.7	5.7
Zeeland	0.9	68.6	4.1

Of the four provinces at the top are two with pronounced Alpine, and two with Nordic population, while the last place is taken by Zeeland which is pronouncedly Alpine.

For the sake of completeness, let it be mentioned that Slingenberg, at the International Anthropological Congress at Prague (1924), gave the following bit of information. Of the accused who appeared during one year before the court

[79] Calculated from the Criminal Statistics for the year 1936, pp. 17–18.

in Amsterdam, 42 percent were of a brunette type, while this type only forms 32 percent of the population.[80]
Table XVIII gives information on Austria.

TABLE XVIII [81]

Provinces	Assault	Rebellion against Authority	Sexual Crimes
	AVERAGE FOR EACH 100,000 OF POPULATION DURING THE YEARS 1895–99 OF CASES OF:		
Bohemia	110	10	3
Tyrol	160	8	13
Lower Austria	162	11	8
Moravia	164	11	6
Vorarlberg	186	9	15
Upper Austria	216	6	10
Salzburg	249	7	9
The Kingdom	250	10	7
Coastland	255	20	5
Silesia	277	9	6
Styria	303	12	10
Dalmatia	305	19	3
Carinthia	307	8	9
Bukowina	390	10	2
Carniola	487	13	6
Galicia	559	7	2

The sections of Austria where the Alpine race is most in evidence (Tyrol, Vorarlberg, Salzburg) show a slight aggressive but a high sexual criminality.

[80] *Coloration capillaire et criminalité* (2d Session de l'Institut International d'Anthropologie à Prague, 1924), pp. 436 ff.
[81] Herz, *Verbrechen und Verbrechertum in Oesterreich*, pp. 28, 30, 33.

To conclude, let us consider the data on Germany (see Table XIX).[82] (For Switzerland nothing can be said, since the Swiss do not record criminal statistics.) In considering subdivisions of German provinces, it appears among other things, that the highest figures, 60.2 and 59.1, are for criminal assault in lower Bavaria and the Palatinate. Sections where the Alpine race is relatively numerous, such as Bavaria and Baden, have high figures, though the east of Germany, where this race is much less numerous, does not differ very much in its rate of aggressive criminality. Other south German provinces, such as Württemberg, Hesse, and also Alsace Lorraine, with a high percentage of Alpines, are just about at the average rate for the country in general.

Thus the facts. They by no means give a uniform impression. It is not possible to say that the Alpine population—or rather the sections where a relatively high percentage of Alpine stock is found—has much higher figures for crime than any other section. One can do no more than speak of a tendency in that direction,—with important exceptions.

In order to explain the criminality in question in regions with a more or less pronounced Alpine population, one can refer, in the first place, to criminal sociology. This study has for some time been able to indicate the chief symptoms in the etiology of aggressive crime, at the same time explaining a large part of sexual crime: neglect and mistreatment of youth, alcoholism, and lack of culture—this latter idea including a number of social factors. To speak very generally, the Alpine population lives in very backward sections

[82] Aschaffenburg, *op. cit.,* pp. 43–46.

Table XIX (Germany)

| Provinces and Districts | OF EACH 10,000 OF POPULATION ABOVE 14 YEARS OF AGE | | | |
| | CRIMINAL ASSAULT | | REBELLION AGAINST AUTHORITY | |
	1903–07	1908–12	1903–07	1908–12
Bavaria	40.0	35.6	3.2	2.8
Baden	33.0	26.7	2.8	3.0
Posen	32.7	28.8	3.8	3.3
East Prussia	32.3	32.8	4.4	4.1
West Prussia	31.6	30.5	5.1	4.6
Silesia	26.5	27.3	5.0	5.4
Rhineland	25.7	21.7	5.5	5.6
Württemberg	24.2	21.1	5.1	5.1
Hesse	24.0	19.0	2.6	1.9
Alsace-Lorraine	23.8	24.0	3.0	3.0
Westphalia	23.5	21.6	4.1	4.3
Pomerania	22.8	20.2	3.5	3.2
The whole (average for) .	22.8	20.4	4.1	3.9
Brandenburg and Berlin ..	16.1	13.9	3.4	2.8
Hesse-Nassau	16.1	13.5	3.6	3.0
Hannover	14.8	14.0	2.8	2.7
Saxonia (province)	13.9	10.5	2.9	2.8
Schleswig-Holstein	10.7	10.5	4.5	5.1
Saxonia (kingdom)	8.0	7.0	5.2	4.2

(agrarian) where great spiritual as well as material poverty is prevalent. In places where this is not the case (for example, Belgium), criminality is not great, and as the material and spiritual welfare increases, crime decreases accordingly.

In his work on crime in Austria, Herz points out that those sections in which aggressive crime is frequent are the retarded ones.

A direct dependence on economic circumstances cannot easily be proved; but indirectly this group of crimes is certainly influenced by economic circumstances. For poverty, which obstructs every aspiring cultural movement, often results in brutality and ignorance. . . . Neglected education, excessive alcoholism bring forward the worst instincts, which are not restrained by self-control and discipline.[83]

Concerning Germany, Aschaffenburg points out that most criminal assaults occur in the three centers where the consumption of alcohol is the largest: in the eastern provinces, in southeast Bavaria, and in the Palatinate, thus among three very different races.[84]

Years ago I explained the very diverse aggressive criminality of the Netherlands by reasons of social milieu, in which no race theory comes into consideration.[85]

Does this mean that we have proved race to be of no importance, on the whole, in the etiology of crime? The author of this study would not want to be responsible for such an hypothesis, although he completely rejects the assertion of Slingenberg that the difference in criminality between persons with light and with dark hair is exclusively a question of race.[86] Aschaffenburg, who, in his explanation, lays the emphasis on social milieu, does not deny the possibility that race is of some importance. "It can also be ad-

[83] *Op. cit.*, p. 28.   [84] *Op. cit.*, p. 48.
[85] *Criminalité et conditions économiques*, p. 719.
[86] *Op. cit.*, p. 445.

mitted that perhaps an unfavorable race mixture gives a great irritability and a tendency to aggressive deeds." [87]

He reports that the inhabitants of the Palatinate have the reputation of being quick and excitable people. Litten points to the same fact in his *Welche sind die soziologischen Ursachen für die Kriminalität in der Rheinpfalz?* [88] Exner ascribes the great difference in aggressive crime between Bavarians and Saxons in a large part to the race factor. "Here lie deep-seated in the people distinctions of character and temperament which must speak out also in the total picture of their criminality." [89] Duynstee mentions race along with social causes, as a factor in the greater criminality of Catholics in the Netherlands. The inhabitants of the southern provinces "are characterized by a much greater liveliness, a stronger urge to express themselves, quicker and more spontaneous reactions to their feelings, etc., just the points which can have influence on their criminality, and, especially in the case of undeveloped and less cultured people, can lead to aggressive crime." [90]

And with this, we come to the psychical side of the race question, in so far as it concerns the Alpines. What is known on this subject? Expectations must not be too high; exact psychological investigations do not exist, as far as I know. As Kretschmer expresses it, "Concerning the spiritual dis-

---

[87] *Op. cit.*, p. 50.   [88] Pages 47 ff.
[89] *Krieg und Kriminalität in Oesterreich*, p. 417.
[90] "De oorzaken van de criminaliteit der Katholieken," *Tijdschrift voor Strafrecht*, XLVII (1937), p. 207. Kempe considers, on the contrary, that "the probability seems very slight that the criminality of the Roman Catholics is influenced strongly by race factors." (*Criminaliteit en Kerkgenootschap*, p. 151.)

position so far as this is a general quality of a race, we are restricted on this point to the judgments and prejudices of individual races directed against each other, which, however, always contain a kernel of truth (else their psychological origin would be scarcely explainable)." [91]

These are more in the nature of impressions, gained from observing the conduct of members of the Alpine race. One must never lose sight of the fact that conduct is always the result of one inherent factor plus two milieu factors (education, etc., plus motive).

Günther, in his *Rassenkunde des deutschen Volkes* [92] asserts that the Alpine race, which he calls "östische Rasse," is characterized by patience, industry and slowness of mentality. The Alpine is a real "Spiessbürger." Easy-going, friendly, and, when intoxicated, "friendly to the point of being obtrusively clinging." He does not quickly become violent, he scolds (!) sooner. In general he does not incline to law-breaking (!). Thus the "portrait parlé" of the Alpine according to the admirer of the Nordic race.

Gault describes the Alpine race as follows: "They are attached to the soil; conservative, peaceful, respectful toward authority, patient, painstaking and democratic. Like the Nordics, they are strongly attached to religion, and are somewhat more liable than they to emotional expression." [93]

Ripley says the following: "A certain passivity, or patience, is characteristic of the Alpine peasantry." "As a rule . . . this Alpine type makes a comfortable and contented neighbor, a resigned and peaceful subject." [94] He adds to

[91] *Geniale Menschen*, p. 79.   [92] Pages 188 ff.
[93] *Criminology*, p. 194.   [94] *The Races of Europe*, pp. 549-50.

this that he cannot determine whether these qualities are innate or result from the milieu. In another place he describes the Welshman as violent in speech, lively of spirit, his feelings easily expressed, more a man of passion than of reason.[95]

Whenever one limits one's self to the characteristics first mentioned by Ripley, in which even emotionality is not named, it would be easy to construe a complete contrast between the criminality and the inherent character of the Alpine. Günther thinks (wrongly) that they show a definitely limited criminality. However it is more accurate to lay the emphasis especially on this last observed quality (emotionality). One can easily multiply the number of opinions about the emotionality of the Alpines. There is no good observer who is not convinced that the people with dark hair and eyes and round heads, speaking very generally, are more emotional and excitable than blonds.

May we conclude from this that the Alpines are more criminally inclined than, for example, the Nordics? The conclusion is unjust. Their disposition is not criminally inclined, it can carry them as well toward good as toward evil. (For instance, toward musicality.) Living under the same criminalistic circumstances, an emotional Nordic will turn sooner to aggressive acts than will his phlegmatic fellow Nordic. If these circumstances are lacking, then this disposition hasn't the least importance. Any reader of this study knows a number of Alpine fellow citizens. Let him ask himself whether these men, when decently brought up and living in comfort and culture, thus averse to crime, can be considered as predisposed to the committing of murder or

[95] *Ibid.*, p. 333.

assault? To ask is to answer; though in the case of persons living in entirely different circumstances, the question would not be ill-founded.

THE CRIMINALITY OF THE NORDICS

The anthropological characteristics of the third great European race, the Nordic, are mainly these: blond hair, blue or grey eyes, dolichocephalic skulls and tall statures. The Nordics are found at their purest and most numerous in the Scandinavian countries: in addition, an important percentage of them is to be met with in north Germany, Holland, Belgium (Flanders), and north France.

Their aggressive and sexual criminality, very generally speaking, is low. This, however, is only true of the present time. Formerly, aggressive criminality was much more prevalent. In the Netherlands, for instance, the rate for aggravated assault in the last thirty years has declined about 50 percent, and assault in England has declined about 66 percent.[96]

A glance at the international statistics given in Table XIV shows that the countries with the strongest Nordic strain come at the very bottom of the list. National statistics indicate much the same thing, though here we note various important exceptions. In Germany (see Table XIX) aggressive criminality is generally low in the northern sections, with the exception of Prussia, where, however, a considerable east Baltic strain is present. In Belgium the aggressive

---

[96] Colajanni, in his *Sociologia criminale* (II, 248 ff.), calls attention to the historical fact that the Scottish, whose aggressive criminality is now so slight, once belonged to the most violent of peoples. The same is true of the Norwegians.

criminality of Flanders, where the Nordic strain is strongest, is greater than that of southern Belgium. In the Netherlands (see Tables XVI and XVII), Friesland is favorably placed, although Drenthe and Groningen have an unfavorable position.

Generally speaking, the slight criminal tendency of the Nordics remains a fact. It is confirmed by figures on the immigrants in the United States, as illustrated in Table XX.

TABLE XX [97]

Countries	CONDEMNED, BY COUNTRY OF BIRTH, PER 100,000 OF POPULATION IN 1910		
	Assault	*Murder*	*Manslaughter*
Mexico	109.6	5.0	11.8
Austria	70.4	1.2	4.0
Italy	67.2	2.3	8.0
Poland	51.9	0.4	1.2
Hungary	49.0	1.2	2.2
Ireland	38.2	0.4	0.8
Russia	36.6	0.1	1.4
All countries	35.5	0.8	2.2
Canada (French)	27.5	0.3	1.0
Scotland	19.9	1.1	0.8
Canada (English)	18.2	0.1	0.7
France	16.2	0.0	2.6
Germany	14.8	0.3	1.0
England and Wales	14.8	0.3	1.5
Sweden	14.4	0.3	0.5
Norway	11.9	0.2	0.7
Denmark	11.6	0.0	1.1
Switzerland	11.2	0.0	1.6

[97] *Prisoners and Juvenile Delinquents in the United States*, 1910, p. 131.

Thus in quite another milieu—to which the immigrants have naturally brought all their previous conceptions, habits, etc.—the Nordics show but a slight tendency to aggressive criminality.

In order to explain the slightness of this criminality, one should really give a sketch of the history of the last three quarters of a century in northern Europe, with emphasis on that of the common people from whom the criminal world is generally recruited. Naturally we cannot begin such a project in this study, it would also be superfluous, since the subject can be studied in other works.[98] Let me only indicate one side of this history. Thanks to the material improvement of the condition of the masses, as well as an improvement in public instruction, the general spiritual level has risen considerably, and with it the standards of culture and ethics. Sport has become an important factor in popular life. The abuse of alcohol has largely disappeared. A rebirth of the people has taken place.

All of this has worked so profoundly that even a large part of the sub-standard group—from which the criminal world in general recruits its worst types—has come up to a level where aggressive crime no longer occurs, or occurs in less serious forms.

The recognition of this fact, which dominates the whole problem, does not relieve us from answering the question as to whether the Nordic race is the same in its psychical disposition as the other European races. This is certainly unlikely. Unfortunately there are no exact psychological in-

[98] I permit myself, in this connection, to call attention to my work, *Criminalité et conditions économiques* (1905), in which such a short sketch is given, in so far as this history is of importance.

vestigations known on the subject, and thus one must be contented with impressions, etc.

If one consults the literature of the subject by the so-called race theorists, who are generally admirers of the Nordics, then it appears that there is nothing better than this race. All the most important and most beautiful things wrought on this terrestrial orb are their works. These authors become positively lyrical when they begin to describe the Nordics. As a result, these expressions cause more mirth than conviction. Love is known to be blind.

For a criminological study, most of these qualities, supposing them to be actually present, are of no importance. "As a thinker, the Nordic man has the will to objectivity and clarity. The classic repose and sobriety of the old Greek and the modern Anglo-Saxon thinker is truly Nordic." says Lenz.[99] Be this true or not—as star witness he drags in Nietzsche, whose "repose and sobriety" is not above suspicion— it has nothing to do with criminology. The only quality which is named by all the writers of this persuasion, and which could be of importance in criminology, is pugnacity. "The inclination to fighting and war is truly Nordic." [100] This does not presage anything good for aggressive criminality. Lenz knows the answer to this, as we have already mentioned. The slight criminality of the Nordic depends on something else again. "The cause of these different ways of behaving can actually lie in the race. Self-discipline, foresight, self-respect, keep the Norse people from lawbreaking." [101]

[99] *Menschliche Erblehre*, 4th edition, p. 742.
[100] *Ibid.*, p. 739.   [101] *Ibid.*, p. 743.

Because of such expressions by presumptuous individuals, one would be inclined to dismiss the whole question. It is better to keep to the opinions of such serious research workers as Ripley and Kretschmer. Their judgment in this case corresponds with the observation of the average man. Among the blonds is a larger percentage of quiet, slow men of non-violent reaction than among the darker people. *That is all.* This temperament is strongly confirmed through education, etc. (strengthening of the secondary function), especially among peoples with an old culture like the English, Scandinavians, and Hollanders.

This is not without importance, from a criminological viewpoint, and it is equally not without importance that the individuals of a single race are not all alike. This (negative) predisposition—no one knows whether it is actually great or not, there being no exact data on the subject—is only harmless under certain circumstances, but harmful under others. It is as dangerous as it would be to go deliberately into an unhygienic milieu in spite of a low resistance to infectious diseases. This can be illustrated by the following example: It is far less dangerous to cross the path of a Mediterranean of lively temperament, but good up-bringing and culture, and unarmed, than that of a Nordic of calm temperament, who has been brought up on thrashings, has remained without culture, never goes out without knife and revolver, and moreover habitually consumes great quantities of alcohol.

THE CRIMINALITY OF THE UGRO-FINNS

At the International Criminal-Anthropological Congress held in Amsterdam in 1901, Tschisch, a professor from Dorpat, gave information on the Esthonians and the Letts.[102] The criminality of the former appears to be much greater than that of the latter. Since, according to the author, the social milieu is the same for both groups, the difference in race should here furnish the explanation.

Weinberg, in his study previously mentioned, agrees with this. He says on the subject:

> The opinion that we are in this case concerned with national and racial characteristics is not without foundation. I am familiar with both races, having been born in that region. From long experience I can say that the Esthonians are in general easily inclined to aggression, which cannot be said for the Letts.
>
> Racially pure Esthonians have confirmed this to me, and therefore I doubt whether certain circumstances of the natural surroundings and economic conditions to which we called attention [here he refers to a study in Russian, by Klossovsky] seriously come in question for those distinctions of character which evidently have their deep biological roots.[103]

Though these peoples (and one must include the Finns as belonging to the same race) have only a modest place in the European concert of races—consisting, as they do, of not more than a few million inhabitants—they are interesting from a criminological point of view.

In 1911 Urbye reported on the criminality of the most northern district of Norway, where Nordics, Lapps, and Finns live. The aggressive and sexual criminality of the Lapps is slight; even under the influence of alcohol they commit few acts of violence. The same can be said for the criminality

---

[102] "La Criminalité comparée des Estes et des Lettoniens" (*Compte rendu du Vme Congrès International d'Anthropologie Criminelle*, 1901, Amsterdam, 1901).

[103] Weinberg, *op. cit.*, p. 724.

of the Nordics: it is, as elsewhere in Norway, slight. That of
the Finns, however, is great. Urbye says of them: "They are
vigorous, cruel natures, given to anger and implacable; they
never forgive an insult or an injury done them. When they
are under the influence of alcohol they are violent, and draw
their knives on the slightest occasion." [104] However, he adds
the following: "By this I do not mean that these things are
generally applicable to all the Finns. It is mainly true of the
wandering Finns who come from Finland to Norway and
move on from place to place, and who also belong to the
lowest class of people in their own country." [105]

In his study "Der Einfluss der Rasse auf die Kriminalität
der Esten" Lellep comes to the same conclusion. He sums up
as follows:

(1) The criminality of the Esthonians can be indicated as a
racial characteristic of an agrarian people endowed with characteristics original to the Ugro-Finnish; (2) Among the Esthonians, rude crimes of passion predominate. (3) In the emotional
make-up of the Ugro-Finnish Esthonians, the excessive use of
alcohol is of very great significance.[106]

Finally, the most distinguished Finnish criminal statistician, Verkko,[107] in his *Verbrechen wider das Leben und
Körperverletzungsverbrechen* informs us that the figure for

[104] "Kriminalität und Rechtspflege im nördlichsten Norwegen," *Zeitschrift für die Strafrechtswissenschaft*, XXXII (1911), 709.
[105] *Ibid.*, p. 709.
[106] *Monatsschrift für Kriminalpsychologie und Strafrechtsreform*,
XVIII (1927).
[107] It is very unfortunate that no publications of Dr. Verkko except this
work have appeared in any of the principal languages of the world. This
is regrettable especially in the case of his work on the connection between aggressive criminality and the character of the people. Dr. Verkko
kindly sent me a detailed résumé in German, a part of which has appeared
in the *Monatsschrift für Kriminalbiologie*, XXIX, 1938, pp. 481 ff.

murders in Finland is about 20 times as high as in the Scandinavian countries.[108] In Finland itself, where about 10 percent of the population speak Swedish, the relative aggressive criminality (manslaughter and assault with resulting death) of the Finnish-speaking part is two or three times as great and, in the case of criminal assault, even four times as great.[109] The figures in Table XIV confirm this.

Now comes the question of how to explain this very divergent criminality—much higher than in Southern Europe! As we have already said, Tschisch, Weinberg, and Lellep, as well as Urbye (to a certain degree), ascribe this to the race. Verkko is also inclined to do this, though he makes important exceptions.

In the first place, this author points out that the enormous aggressive criminality of the Finns is explained by alcoholism, which is very prevalent among them. From an investigation made in 1931 on the causes of the increase in criminality in the years 1920–29, this appears to be the case. Table XXI gives the details.

In the United States, also, the Finns, of all immigrants, are found guilty of the most misdemeanors while under the influence of alcohol (see Table XXII).

This table shows, at the same time, that the other Scandinavian peoples are also guilty to a great extent of misdemeanors while under the influence of alcohol, although in their case this does not lead (as shown in Table XX) to serious aggressive criminality. This would confirm the remark by Lellep that alcohol causes different reactions in different races. It has long been known to be the case with different individ-

[108] Pages 122–23.   [109] *Ibid.*, p. 488.

TABLE XXI (FINLAND) [110]

	Intoxicated at the Moment of the Crime (Percent)	Had Consumed Small Quantity of Alcohol on the Day of Crime (Percent)
Murderers	7.26	14.11
Committed manslaughter or assault which resulted in death	62.06	14.91
Committed criminal assault ...	66.91	13.22
Committed acts of violence resulting in death or serious injury	53.37	13.50

uals in a single race.[111] Since the Finns are not mentioned in Table XX—probably because they had not migrated at that time in sufficient numbers to the United States—let us here state, for the sake of completeness, that later figures show that the Finns take fourth place in the case of disorderly conduct, fifth in the case of manslaughter, and eighth, or average, place in cases of assault.[112]

Verkko also mentions a number of social factors which influence the rate of Finnish aggressive crime, in addition to the race factor. The following passage is taken from a résumé in my possession of his great work.

Factors working against the Finns have been protracted wars and turbulent times. In respect to these, Finland has found itself in a more difficult situation during hundreds of years than, for instance, her nearest neighbor, Sweden. But certain

---

[110] *Ibid.*, p. 497.
[111] It would be extremely interesting if a laboratory test could establish the difference in reaction to alcohol of the various races and types.
[112] *Monatsschrift für Kriminalbiologie*, XXIX, 486–87.

TABLE XXII [113]

NUMBER OF IMMIGRANTS CONVICTED, BETWEEN JAN. 1 AND JUNE
30, 1923, FOR MISDEMEANORS WHILE DRUNK; IN PRISON
BECAUSE THEY WERE UNABLE TO PAY THE FINE

Countries	Absolute Total	Per 100,000 of Each Group
Finland	733	489.2
Ireland	2,528	243.7
Norway	703	193.2
Sweden	1,107	117.0
Scotland	313	123.0
Mexico	529	110.6
Austria	521	90.5
Poland	878	77.1
Canada	790	70.7
Russia	619	44.2
Hungary	169	42.5
England and Wales	351	39.9
Germany	290	17.2
Greece	25	14.2
Italy	208	12.9

prominent sides of the Finnish character are likewise not without significance. Slowness of reaction, reticence, autocratic manner, tenacity; these are the negative sides of the Finnish character, according to general observation. In the alcohol reaction, these characteristics cause a sudden outburst, bringing to the surface old grievances, and provoking fights. It is interesting to note that a most important difference exists between the kind of aggressive crime committed by the east and by the west Finns. Among the former, the crimes brought about by alcohol are less numerous, and this part of the Finns

[113] *Ibid.*, p. 486.

is also, as is generally known, of another nature than the west Finns. They are more playful and animated and adapt themselves more easily to the community than the others. Of greater importance also is the bootleg product which became quite general in the time of the prohibition law (1919–1931) in Finland, namely distilled liquor.

The general conclusion of Verkko on the influence of race is expressed in the following words: "Naturally the hereditary racial qualities are a factor in the forming of people's character and custom, but their influence is not so deciding as one would be inclined to conclude from a first glance at the statistical comparisons."

Although in all the quoted opinions on the aggressive criminality of the Finns and Esthonians the proposition that this depends partially on the races in question is actually based on a diagnosis by elimination (a diagnosis not considered very valuable by the medical profession), the great possibility cannot be denied that the proposition contains an element of truth. Apparently these peoples [114] who are more aggressive than others by nature—but in a quite different manner from the Mediterraneans—react in this way to alcohol. A thorough experimental investigation, such as bringing up a large number of these children in another land and in a totally different atmosphere, would establish whether this difference is really great.

To label an aggressive disposition as criminal does not appeal to me, as I have said before. Circumstances conducive to crime must be assumed, otherwise this disposition has noth-

[114] From the anthropological works known to me, I have not been able to determine to what race they belong. The Letts are Nordics, the Esthonians and Finns also, but with another strain (Mongoloid?). The language of the latter is related to the Hungarian.

ing to do with criminology. The refined, cultured, substantial Finns—who certainly do not carry knives or revolvers—are surely as little given to committing acts of violence as any similar group of non-Finns.

THE CRIMINALITY OF THE EAST BALTICS AND OTHERS

For the sake of completeness, the East Baltic race will also be mentioned, although we are not in a position here to give much information from a criminological point of view. The East Baltics are blond, brachycephalic, thick-set, powerful people. They inhabit central Russia and a section of Poland; they have crowded into eastern Germany, and have mixed with the Nordics.

So far as I know, Tarnowski [115] was the first to publish data in a western language on Russian criminal statistics. Only in his *Repartition géographique de la criminalité en Russie* [116] is there any information (concerning the years 1895–97) on the question which occupies us. He notes, namely, that the central portion of Russia has a comparatively slight criminality, which grows greater toward the periphery. Some think that this depends on "the innate gentleness of the Russian people and on its natural morality, which is far greater than that of other peoples." [117] Tarnowski calls this a nationalistic point of view and does not accept it. There are sections of central Russia where crime flourishes (Prov-

[115] See his "Le Mouvement de la criminalité en Russie," *Archives d'Anthropologie Criminelle*, XIII (1898) and "La delinquenza e la vita sociale in Russie," *Rivista Italiana di Sociologia*, II (1898).
[116] *Archives d'Anthropologie Criminelle*, XVI (1901).
[117] Page 118.

ince of Moscow) and others where the crime rate is but slight, where few Russians live. Besides, he emphatically denies that the passive, resigned character of the Russian moujik is inherent.

Verkko in his work previously mentioned: *Verbrechen wider das Leben und Körperverletzungsverbrechen,* and in the book which is outlined in the *Monatsschrift,* gives figures on the criminality in Russia for the period 1899–1914. From this it would appear in the first place that aggressive criminality in Russia is great, in a general comparison with the surrounding countries, including Finland, and therefore should have a place at the top of the list in Table XIV. In the second place, that the great amount of aggressive crime in Asiatic Russia, where numerous other peoples and races live under quite different conditions, is far greater than in European Russia.

If one divides European Russia, in the customary way, into three great sections: Russia proper, Russian Poland, and the Caucasus, then the last named territory has the maximum of serious aggressive crime (five or six times greater than Russia proper), Poland follows, and the minimum is found in Russia proper.

In his other study (in Finnish) Verkko does not base his work on the indirect (geographical) method, but on direct data (see Table XXIII). The Russians proper take the middle place here. Figures on America (Table XX) confirm this.

To what extent the criminality of the East Baltics in Russia has any connection with their inherent characteristics is a question which cannot be answered in the present state of our sociological and psychological knowledge.

TABLE XXIII [118]

Nationalities	Crimes against Human Life, 1908–12	All Forms of Assault, 1908–12
	(Per 100,000 pop.)	
Armenians	16.0	4.6
Caucasian mountain people	14.8	4.8
Georgians, etc.	10.4	4.6
Turk-Tartars (1908)	6.0	3.0
Russians	4.0	6.2
Poles	3.8	12.2
Lithuanians and Letts	3.4	5.4
Germans	2.0	2.4
Jews	1.4	2.4

In conclusion, here are some observations on the criminality of the Poles. This people belongs only partially to the East Baltic race—anthropology teaches that the Poles belong to six races.[119] From the data of Verkko on former Russian Poland, it appears that aggressive criminality was extensive there, in the case of assault even very extensive. The same is true for what was formerly German Poland, as is shown in Table XIX, where the four provinces with a Polish strain belong to the most strongly criminal in Germany. In the United States (see Table XX) the Polish take a large place among those guilty of assault. On the other hand, in the most serious forms of aggressive criminality they have a slighter share. It appears from the post-war figures

[118] *Monatsschrift für Kriminalpsychologie und Strafrechtsreform,* XXIX (1939), 489.
[119] The so-called Slavic race is not a separate race. "Slavic" applies to a language group.

(see Table XIV) that murder and manslaughter is very frequent in Poland, 7.3 per 100,000 of population as against 0.5 in the Netherlands.

The explanation of this, as we might expect, creates no difficulties for a number of German authors. For them the Polish race (which one?) is the true cause of guilt. Galle, for example, in his study *Untersuchungen über die Kriminalität in der Provinz Schlesien*, ascribes the high degree of criminality in some sections of this province to the great number of Poles living there. ". . . we can certainly accept that it is the Polish character qualities which cause the high rate of criminality." [120]

Stöwesand observes, in his *Die Kriminalität in der Provinz Posen und ihre Ursachen*, that sections of the province where the Polish population increased considerably saw a like increase in aggressive criminality. He writes:

These reappearing phenomena however, cause one to conclude that the Poles apparently carry the blame for the increase in criminality. Their characteristic qualities confirm this. The Pole is pictured by all authorities as fawning and quarrelsome. Of a powerful build and great skill, he is animated and easily irritated, unrestrained and passionate.[121]

Other authors, however, doubt the importance of the race factor and point to the very low economic and cultural level of the Poles. Aschaffenburg denies that the great aggressive criminality in the east of Germany can be ascribed to race, although he does not deny the possibility of this.

One thing we can assert with certainty: that the possible existing racial differences exert a very small influence on the total

[120] *Der Gerichtssaal,* LXXII (1908), 109.
[121] Page 86.

criminal manifestation of the inhabitants, as opposed to the great significance of the popular welfare and national customs. The strong share of the East in Germany's criminality does not so soon point to the absence of morals in the population, as to bad economic conditions and to deplorable habits of life.[122]

Peterselie, also, in his *Untersuchungen über die Kriminalität in der Provinz Sachsen* (there are Polish elements in parts of this province), Bessler in his *Die Kriminalität Westpreussens*, and von Hentig in his *Die schwere Kriminalität in Preussen 1910–1912* express themselves very cautiously on this question. Von Hentig says:

The question of whether the high rate of criminality among the Poles is a racial quality or whether it is to be blamed on the sharp action of the persecuting officials, or the lessened capacity for legal defense due to poverty, ignorance, and ignorance of the language, is not to be decided without further evidence. But there is much which indicates that the financial circumstances, a certain unpopularity as a race, and the lack of culture are not without influence.[123]

Exner, also, in his *Volkscharacter und Verbrechen* observes the presence of much crime in the sections of east Germany where Polish minorities live, and the fact that this has decreased since the frontier has been changed. He is in doubt about the exact role of race in this phenomenon. ". . . the Slavic people who have settled in Germany have an exceptionally low cultural and economic standard. It is not possible to say with certainty whether their increased criminality comes from their national character. The probability is that this is so." [124] Verkko also ascribes the serious aggressive

[122] *Op. cit.*, p. 57.
[123] *Monatsschrift für Kriminalpsychologie und Strafrechtsreform*, XI (1914), 135.
[124] *Op. cit.*, XXIX (1938), 414.

criminality of the Poles to the generally very great use of alcohol, though he adds that they have an "aufwallendes Temperament und eine streitsüchtige Natur."

Since I lack the data on the inherent character of the Poles (I doubt whether such data exist) I shall not venture to give a definite opinion on them, and the situation must remain unclear. Presumably it is not inexact to state that the Poles are of an emotional nature—to what extent naturally no one knows—and emotional people are more predisposed to aggressive acts than non-emotional ones. Emotionality also naturally predisposes to quite different sorts of deeds, and it is therefore quite unjustified to qualify emotion as a factor in crime. Under certain criminalistic circumstances, and these appear to be amply present in the lowest stratum of Polish society, this emotionality is not altogether without significance.

CHAPTER IV

Résumé and Conclusion

W̲ᴇ ʜᴀᴠᴇ already anticipated one conclusion reached in the Foreword: that no definite results have been obtained in the study of "race and crime," and that much still remains unsettled. This conclusion, as I see it, was well founded. The more arbitrarily some writers express themselves on the subject, the more a skeptical attitude is justified.

The reasons for this lie in various fields. The anthropology of races is still only in its inception, and its conclusions, which especially concern anatomic phenomena, are of little or no significance for criminology. The study of the anatomy of the brain, particularly, has not yet been far enough advanced to explain the differences among races which might exist on this point. Precisely this branch of anthropology which deals with something genuinely inherent would be of the greatest significance in this matter.

Thus we are lacking much, if not all, information on the material side of the problem; and in the case of the psychology of races the situation is not much better. On this point especially we are still obliged to rely on impressions and the like, in which scientific control is impossible. These impressions often come from superficial observers who, besides being full of prejudices, are all too inclined to consider the qualities observed by them as inherent. Only a thoroughgoing research, however, can separate inheritance from environment.

Scientific psychology has indeed occupied itself with races. It has not yet gone very far however, though a promising beginning has been made. Its results lie principally in the sphere of the intelligence, which is of secondary importance for criminology; while in the research in character, so important to our subject, it is as yet but slightly advanced. Expectations for the future of this latter research should not be too high, since the character lends itself badly to experimentation, and, in the main, is only "tested" in real life. The best results until now have been obtained in the sphere of the temperament, where the influences of milieu are of less importance and can still best be eliminated. When the psychiatry of races has made greater advances than is now the case (though a promising beginning has also been made in this field), then important results can likewise be expected from it for the criminology of races.

Though the study of criminology is not yet widely supported by other branches of natural science, it must confess that in its own field it is also badly informed about "race and crime." This is especially true in the question: How extensive is crime in the various races? Criminal statistics is an institution which until now has been found principally in countries with white populations, so that, to begin with, two principal races (yellow and black) must remain quite outside consideration. The quite accidental fact that a part of the Negroes live in the United States makes it possible to learn at least something of their criminality in that milieu.

When we limit ourselves to the white race, then criminal statistics again leave us in the dark with our problem. Namely, they do not mention the race to which the delinquents belong—with a single insignificant exception. Once more it is an accident that in the case of the Jews religion and race more or less coincide, and thus in a roundabout way one can account for that race. For the rest, we have recourse only to geographical comparison by which we can amass data about race only indirectly, incompletely and imperfectly. The very great racial mixture makes the basis for the drawing of comparisons even more unsure.

So far as the theoretical basis of the problem is concerned, it has become certain that criminality is not a characteristic such as the possession of a round skull, blue eyes, or musicality—those characteristics in which races differ. Consequently, to speak of criminal races (in which all the individuals would be criminal) is pure nonsense. No person comes into the world a criminal (if one omits consideration of pathological cases—*insania moralis*). Crime is always limited to a (comparatively) small number of individuals in a race. The proposed question must thus be expressed otherwise: Does one race more than another count a greater or lesser number of variants in certain qualities, and do they then also differ in their averages, which could be significant in one way or another for criminology?

The races differ—this may well be taken as positive—not alone physically but also psychically. That they differ in the whole psychical sphere is highly improbable. On the contrary, it is possible that in several respects they are alike. Differences, for example, in fantasy, in musicality—in the sense that one race has a greater number of variants in this field than another—may well be taken as positive. Arising from these differences, the question, a very important one, is now put: How great are these differences? Two races can differ in the number of variants, but it is very important whether this percentage is, say, between two and three, or between twenty and thirty. The author of this study is firmly convinced that there are differences among the races, but he has nearly as strong a suspicion that they are sorely exaggerated.

Many psychical qualities are irrelevant to criminology, others can be significant. Query: Is this evident from the facts?

First of all, the most flagrant contradiction is sometimes witnessed between criminological facts and what is psychologically known. The Nordic race is pictured, for example, as being violent in its inherent nature, but its aggressive criminality is (with exceptions!) small. The Jewish race, to take another example, numbers very probably a greater percentage of nervous cases than others, but it counts few crimes of violence, although the "nervous type" is somewhat predisposed to this sort of crime.

On the other hand, there are cases in which there is indeed agreement between criminological and psychological facts. We limit ourselves to the temperament, very nearly the only fact about which we may speak with any certainty. (There is, for instance, not the least shadow of evidence that races show a congenital dishonesty.) As an example, and a striking one, we choose the aggressive criminality of the Mediterraneans. This is great, and their temperament is quick and violent. (Naturally this is only true *in general;* the breadth of variation within *one* race is ordinarily great, so that one section of a naturally non-violent race is more violent than one section of a naturally violent race: "over-lapping curves.") Here, as I see it, one can speak of a certain predisposition, just as this is the case within *one* race where the individuals likewise differ in temperament.

Has one the right, now, to qualify this predisposition as criminal? As I see it, this question must be answered emphatically in the negative. *There is no question of special predisposition for crime.* A lively, violent disposition also predisposes to other deeds, least of all to crime. The phlegmatic type (to name the opposite temperament) are worthy, dutiful burghers in general, but the pioneers of mankind mostly do not belong to this type. In other words, it becomes a question of the circumstances under which a man has lived from birth, and under which he still lives. A choleric temperament is dangerous under quite other conditions. In this connection it is important to remark that female criminality is generally slight in lands where aggressive crime is frequent, although the women belong to the same race as the men.

Predisposition is not predestination. The enormous differences in criminality within one race show this—differences which are due to education, well-being, culture and all that goes with it. The great changes which criminality has undergone within *one* race in the course of time under the influence of changing circumstances show this as well.

The simple truth that predisposition is not predestination is well known to medical hygiene. The predisposition to catch one of the most serious infectious diseases (cholera, for instance) is great, perhaps greater in general than that to become a criminal. This predisposition, no doubt a special one, is also various for different individuals: some catch the disease sooner than others, as the history of epidemics has taught us. In the civilized world, however, hygiene has known how to create conditions such that no one, not even the strongly predisposed, any longer catches this dread disease. As soon as these conditions had been reached no one was any longer interested in the question: Of what nature is this predisposition?

Since medical hygiene is considerably more advanced than her sister in criminology, they are miles separated from each other in practice. And it is to be feared that such will long be the case. In principle, however, there is no difference between the two.

Bibliography

This bibliography consists of the titles listed by Bonger, and of many other titles mentioned in the text; also the titles of whatever English translations of these books I could find, and of other English translations of works by these authors when they appear to have a bearing on the subject at hand. (Translator's note.)

Abbreviations used:
American Journal (American Journal of Sociology)
Archiv (Archiv für Kriminalanthropologie und Kriminalistik, later Archiv für Kriminologie)
Archives (Archives d'Anthropologie Criminelle)
Journal (Journal of Criminal Law and Criminology)
Monatsschrift (Monatsschrift für Kriminalpsychologie und Strafrechtsreform)
Tijdschrift (Tijdschrift voor Strafrecht)
Zeitschrift (Zeitschrift für Demographie und Statistik der Juden)

Adams, H. L., The Indian Criminal, London, 1909.
—— Oriental Crime, London, 1908.
Ambrunn, L., "Die Kriminalität der Juden in Russland," *Zeitschrift*, II (1906), and V (1909).
Amir, Dr. M., "Constitutietypen bij crimineelen, *Geneeskundig Tijdschrift voor Nederlandsch Indië*, LXXIV (1934).
—— "De inheemse psychopathen en hunne sociale beteekenis, *Koloniale Studiën*, XVII (1933).
—— "Over inheemse psychopathen en hunne forensische beteekenis," *Geneeskundig Tijdschrift voor Nederlandsch Indië*, LXXIV (1934).
Ammoun, Fouad, La Syrie criminelle, Paris, 1929.
Arène, S., De la criminalité des Arabes au point de vue de la pratique médico-judiciaire en Tunisie, Valence, 1913.
Arrii, D. C., De l'impulsivité criminelle chez l'indigène Algérien, Alger, 1926.

Aschaffenburg, G., Das Verbrechen und seine Bekämpfung, Heidelberg, 1906, 3d ed., 1923.

—— Crime and Its Repression, Boston, Little, Brown, 1913.

Avé-Lallement, F. C. B., Das deutsche Gaunerthum in socialen, politischen, literarischen, und linguistischen Ausbildung, Leipzig, 1858–62.

Barge, J. A. J. *See* Steinmetz, Barge, Hagedoorn, and Steinmetz.

Beach, W. G., Oriental Crime in California; a Study of Offenses Committed by Orientals in That State, Palo Alto, Calif., 1932.

Bernheim, Ernst, Lehrbuch der historischen Methode und der Geschichtsphilosophie, Leipzig, 1908.

Bertholon, Lucien, "Esquisse de l'anthropologie criminelle des Tunisiens musulmans," *Archives,* IV (1889).

Bessler, K., Die Kriminalität Westpreussens, Breslau, 1915.

Bijlmer, H. J. T., Anthropological Results of a Dutch Scientific Central New Guinea Expedition. Leiden, 1922.

—— Naar de achterhoek der aarde. 1938.

—— "Rassen en kruisingen," in *Erfelijkheid bij de mens,* IV (1925).

Blau, B., "Der Einfluss des Antisemitismus auf die Gestaltung der Kriminalstatistik, *Zeitschrift,* II (1906).

—— Die Kriminalität der deutschen Juden, Berlin, 1906.

—— "Die Kriminalität der Juden in Deutschland während der Jahre 1903–1906, *Zeitschrift,* V (1909).

—— "Die Kriminalität der Juden in Preussen im Jahre 1910," *Zeitschrift,* IX (1913).

Boas, Franz, Kultur und Rasse, Leipzig, 1914. (English title, *The Mind of Primitive Man.*)

—— The Mind of Primitive Man, New York, 1938.

Böckle, Der Juden Antheil am Verbrechen, Berlin, 1881.

Bolk, Louis, "De bevolking van Nederland in hare anthropologische samenstelling, in Gallée, *Das niederländische Bauernhaus* . . . which see.

Bonger, Adriaan, Criminalité et conditions économiques. Amsterdam, 1905.

Bonger, Adriaan, Criminality and Economic Conditions. Boston, 1915.

—— Geloof en misdaad. Leiden, 1913.

—— Inleiding tot de criminologie. 1932.

—— An Introduction to Criminology. London, 1936.

—— "Misdaad en socialisme," *Nieuwe Tijd*, XVI (1911).

—— "De oorlog als sociologisch probleem, *Socialistische Gids*, XV (1930); also published separately.

—— "Over Criminele Statistiek," *Tijdschrift voor Strafrecht*, XLVIII (1938).

Botti, E., La delinquenza femminile a Napoli. Napoli, 1904.

Boule, Marcellin, Les Hommes fossiles. Paris, 1921.

—— Fossil Men. Edinburgh, 1923.

Bournet, A., De la criminalité en France et en Italie. Paris, 1884.

Braconnier, A. de, De Kinderkriminaliteit in Nederlandsch Indië. Baarn, 1918.

Broek, A. J. P. van den, "De anthropologische samenstelling der bevolking van Nederland," *Mensch en Maatschappij*, VI (1930).

Cardozo, D. S. Jessurun, "Aanteekeningen over onze criminaliteit" (I), *Joodsch Hulpbetoon*, I (1933).

Chamberlain, H. S., Die Grundlagen der XIX Jahrhunderts. 1899.

—— Foundations of the 19th Century. New York, 1913.

Cheinisse, L., "Die Rassenpathologie und der Alkoholismus bei den Juden," *Zeitschrift*, VI (1910).

Claghorn, K., "Crime and Immigration," *Journal of Criminal Law and Criminology*, VIII (1917–18).

Colajanni, N., "L'Homicide en Italie," *Revue Socialiste, XVII* (1901).

—— La sociologia criminale, II, Catania, 1889.

Corre, Armand, Le Crime en pays créoles. Lyon; Paris, 1889.

—— Crime et suicide. Paris, 1891.

—— L'Ethnographie criminelle. Paris, 1894.

—— "Facteurs généraux de la criminalité dans les pays créoles," *Archives,* IV (1889).

Cox, E. C., Police and Crime in India. London, 1911.

Culver, D. C., Bibliography of Crime and Criminal Justice (University of California), 1927–1931, 1934; 1932–1937, 1939.

Deniker, Joseph, Les Races et les peuples de la terre. 2d ed. Paris, 1926.

—— The Races of Man. New York, 1927.

Dowd, Jerome, The Negro in American Life. New York, 1927.

Durkheim, Emile, Le Suicide. Paris, 1897.

Duynstee, W. J. A. J., "De oorzaken van de criminaliteit der Katholieken," *Tijdschrift*, XLVII (1937).

Edwardes, S. M., Crime in India. London; New York, 1924.

Enthoven, F. B., "De Lynchwet in de Vereenigde Staten van Noord-America," *Tijdschrift*, XV (1903).

Ettinger, S., Das Verbrecherproblem in anthropologischer und sociologischer Beleuchtung, I, Bern, 1909.

Exner, F., Krieg und Kriminalität in Oesterreich. 1927.

—— "Volkscharakter und Verbrechen," *Monatsschrift*, XXIX (1938).

Fano, G., "Criminali e prostitute in Oriente," *Archivio di Psichiatria, Scienze penali ed Anthropologia criminale*, XV (1894).

Feber, G. H. A., De criminaliteit der Katholieken in Nederland. 1933.

Fehlinger, K., "Die amerikanische Gefängnisstatistik vom Jahre 1904," *Archiv*, XXX (1908).

—— "Die Kriminalität der Neger in den Vereinigten Staaten," *Archiv*, XXIV (1906).

—— "Die Kriminalität in den Vereinigten Staaten," *Archiv*, LXXI (1919).

Fernald, M. R., M. H. S. Hayes, and A. Dawley, A Study of Women Delinquents in New York State. New York, 1920.

Ferri, Enrico, Sociologie criminelle. Paris, 1893; 1905.

—— Criminal Sociology. Boston, 1909.

Fischer, E., "Spezielle Anthropologie: Rassenlehre," in Anthropologie. Leipzig and Berlin, 1923.

Forel, Auguste, Die Sexuelle Frage. Munich, 1913.
—— The Sexual Question. New York, 1922.
Fouillée, Alfred, Tempérament et caractère. Paris, 1895.
Frets, G. P. Heredity of the Head-Form in Man. The Hague, 1921.
—— "Het rassenvraagstuk," *Socialistische Gids*, XIX (1934).
Fuld, Ludwig, Das jüdische Verbrecherthum. Leipzig, 1885.
Galle, J., "Untersuchungen über die Kriminalität in der Provinz Schlesien," *Der Gerichtssaal*, LXXII (1908).
Gallée, J. H., Das niederländische Bauernhaus und seine Bewohner. Utrecht, 1907; Dutch translation, 1908.
Garofalo, R., La Criminologie. Paris, 1890; 1895.
—— Criminology. Boston, 1914.
Garth, T. R., Race Psychology. New York, 1931.
Gault, R. H. Criminology. New York, 1932.
Giardini, G., "A Report on the Italian Convict," in Root, A Psychological and Educational Survey . . . which see.
Ginsberg, Morris, Sociology. London, 1934.
Gobineau, J. A., Essai sur l'inégalité des races humaines. 1853.
—— The Inequality of Human Races. New York, 1915.
Goetz, W. W., "Rasse und Geschichte," in Rasse und Geist, Leipzig, 1932.
Goldberg, B., "Zur Kriminalität der Juden im Russland," *Zeitschrift*, VIII (1912).
Göring, M. H., Kriminalpsychologie. München, 1922.
Grant, Madison, The Passing of the Great Race. New York, 1916.
Guégo, Henry, Contribution à l'étude statistique sur la criminalité en France de 1826 à 1900. Paris, 1902.
Günther, H. F., The Racial Elements of European History London, 1927.
—— Rassenkunde des deutschen Volkes. 1922.
Hacker, Ervin, Der Einfluss der Konfession auf die Kriminalität in Ungarn. Miskolc, 1930.

Hacker, Ervin, "Statistique comparée de la criminalité," *Revue Internationale de Droit Pénal*, XIII (1936).

Haikerwal, Bejay S., Economic and Social Aspects of Crime in India. London, 1934.

Hamnett, G. C., Deletti femminile a Napoli. Milano, 1896.

Handwörterbuch der Kriminologie, II, 4 vols. Berlin, 1932; Berlin and Leipzig, 1936.

Hankins, F. H., The Racial Basis of Civilization. 1926.

Hayner, N. S., "Social Factors in Oriental Crime," *American Journal*, XLIII (1937–38).

Haynes, F. E., Criminology. New York, 1930, 1935.

Henderson, C. R., Introduction to the Study of Dependent, Defective, and Delinquent Classes. Boston, 1909.

Hentig, Hans von, "Die Kriminalität des Negers," *Schweizerische Zeitschrift für Strafrecht*, LII (1938–39).

—— Punishment, Its Origin, Purpose, Psychology. London, 1937.

—— "Die schwere Kriminalität in Preussen, 1910–1912," *Monatsschrift*, XI (1914).

Hersch, L., Le Juif délinquant. Paris, 1938.

Hertz, F. O., Moderne Rassentheorien. Vienna, 1904.

—— Race and Civilization. London, 1928.

Hertz, Friedrich, "Die schwarze Gefahr in Amerika," *Socialistische Monatshefte*, IX (1905).

Herz, H., "Die Kriminalität der Juden in Oesterreich," *Archiv für Strafrecht*, LIV (1907).

—— Verbrechen und Verbrechertum in Oesterreich. Tübingen, 1908.

Hirschfeld, Magnus, Geschlechtskunde, II, Stuttgart, 1930.

Hoegel, H., "Die Grenzen der Kriminalstatistik," *Statistische Monatshefte*, N.F. XII (1907).

Hoppe, Hugo, Alkohol und Kriminalität. Wiesbaden, 1906.

—— "Die Kriminalität der Juden und der Alkohol," *Zeitschrift*, III (1907).

Houzé, Emile, L'Aryen et l'anthroposociologie. Bruxelles, 1906.

Jacobowski, L., Der Juden Anteil am Verbrechen. Berlin, 1892.

Jacquart, C., La Criminalité Belge 1868–1909. Louvain, 1912.

Jhering, Rudolf von, Der Zweck im Recht. Leipzig, 1884.

Kastein, G. W., Het Rassenvraagstuk. 1938.

Kautsky, Karl, Rasse und Judentum. 1914.

—— Are the Jews a Race? New York, 1926.

Kempe, G. T., Criminaliteit en kerkgenootschap. Nijmegen, 1938.

Klaatsch, Hermann, "Die niederen Menschenrassen in ihrer Bedeutung für die Kriminalistik," *Die Umschau*, XV (1911).

—— The Evolution and Progress of Mankind. London, 1923.

—— Die Morphologie und Psychologie der niederen Menschenrassen in ihrer Bedeutung für die Probleme der Kriminalistik. (*Bericht ü.d. VII International Kongress für kriminal Anthropologie*, Köln, 1911, Heidelberg, 1912).

Klineberg, O., Negro Intelligence. New York, 1935.

—— Race Differences. New York and London, 1935.

Kocher, A., De la criminalité chez les Arabes. Paris, 1884.

Kohlbrugge, J. F. H., Blikken in het zieleleven van den Javaan en zijner overheersers. 1907.

Kolaly, M. El, Essai sur les causes de la criminalité actuelle en Egypte. Paris, 1929.

Kovalewsky, Paul, La Psychologie criminelle. Paris, 1903.

Kretschmer, Ernest, Geniale Menschen. Berlin, 1929.

—— "Genie und Rasse," in Rasse und Geist, Leipzig, 1932.

—— The Psychology of Men of Genius. London and New York, 1931.

Kuhlmann, A. F., A Guide to Material on Crime and Criminal Justice. New York, 1929.

Kurella, H., Naturgeschichte des Verbrechers. Stuttgart, 1893.

Lapouge, Vacher de, L'Aryen; son rôle social. Paris, 1899.

Leers, Johann von, "Die Kriminalität des Judentums," in *Das Judentum in der Rechtswissenschaft*, No. 3, Judentum und Verbrechen, Berlin, n.d.

Lellep, C., "Der Einfluss der Rasse auf die Kriminalität der Esten," *Monatsschrift*, XVIII (1927).

Lenz, F., "Die Erblichkeit der geistigen Eigenschaften," in E. Baur, E. Fischer, F. Lenz, *Menschliche Erblehre*. 4th ed. Munich (1936).

—— Human Heredity. New York, 1931.

Leydesdorff, J., Bijdrage tot de Speciale Psychologie van het Joodse Volk. 1919.

Liszt, F. von, Das Problem der Kriminalität der Juden. Geissen, 1907.

Litten, K., Welche sind die soziologischen Ursachen für die Kriminalität in den Rheinpfalz. Charlottenburg, 1928.

Lombroso, C., Le Crime; causes et remèdes. Paris, 1899.

—— Crime, Its Causes and Remedies. Boston, 1911; 1918.

—— Neue Verbrecherstudien. Halle, 1907.

Loon, F. H. van, De psychische Eigenschappen der Maleische Rassen, (Report of the Indische Genootschap, The Hague, 1924).

—— "Rassenpsychologische onderzoekingen," *Psychiatrische en Neurologische Bladen*, XXXII (1928).

—— and G. Papillaut, "L'Organisation de l'étude comparative de la psychologie des races," Congress of the International Institute of Anthropology, Amsterdam, 1927.

Lorion, L., Criminalité et médicine judiciaire en Cochin-Chine. Lyon, 1887.

Löwenfeld, S., Die Wahrheit über der Juden Antheil am Verbrechen. Berlin, 1881.

Lux, H., Die Juden als Verbrecher. München, 1894.

McDougall, W., An Introduction to Social Psychology. 1908; 6th ed. 1921.

Manouvrier, L., "L'Indice céphalique et la pseudo-sociologie," *Revue de l'École d'Anthropologie* (1899).

Manzini, V., Le varie specie di furto nella storia e nella sociologia, III, Torino, 1913.

Martin, R. L., Rasse und Verbrechen. Giessen, 1937.

Matignon, J. J., Superstition, crime et misère en Chine. Lyon, 1902.

Matteoti, G., La recidiva. Torino, 1910.

Mayr, Georg von, Statistik und Gesellschaftslehre, III, Tübingen, 1917.

Meihuizen, J., "Een enkel woord over de mate, waarin zich de verschillende bevolkingsgroepen in ons Leger verhouden op het gebied der criminaliteit," *Indisch Militair Tijdschrift*, XLVIII (1916).

Mezger, Edmond, Kriminalpolitik. Stuttgart, 1934.

Mikorey, M., "Das Judentum in der Kriminalpsychologie," *Das Judentum in der Rechtswissenschaft*, No. 3, Judentum und Verbrechen, Berlin, n.d.

Mok, S., "Godsdienst en misdadigheid," *Socialistische Gids*, XXIII (1938).

Morrison, W. D., Crime and Its Causes. London, 1908.

Müller-Lyer, F. C., Der Sinn des Lebens und die Wissenschaft. Munich, 1910.

Murchison, C., Criminal Intelligence. Worcester, 1926.

—— "The Literacy of Negro Men Criminals," *Pedagogical Seminary*, XXXII (1925).

Murchison, C., and Burfield, H., "Types of Crime and Intelligence of Negro Criminals," *Pedagogical Seminary*, XXXII (1925).

Murchison, C., and R. Gilbert, "Some Occupational Concomitants of Negro Men Criminals," *Pedagogical Seminary*, XXXII (1925).

Naecke, P., "Rasse und Verbrechen," *Archiv*, XXV (1906).

Nathanson, H., "Die Kriminalität der Juden und Nichtjuden in Ungarn in den Jahren 1906–9," *Zeitschrift*, VII (1911).

Nicolai, H., Rasse und Recht, Berlin, 1933.

Nieuwenhuis, A. W., "De Veranlagung der malaiischen Völker des Ostindischen Archipels, *International Archiv für Ethnographie*, XXI (1913).

Nina-Rodrigues, Raymundo, "Métissage, dégénérescence, et crime, *Archives*, XIV (1899).

Notes on Negro Crime (Atlanta University Bulletin, No. 9, 1904).

Oppenheimer, Franz, "Die Rassentheoretische Geschichtsphilosophie," (Verhandlungen des 2en deutschen Soziologentages, 1912).

——— The State: Its History and Development Viewed Sociologically. Indianapolis, 1914; London, 1923.

——— System der Soziologie, I. Jena, 1922–35.

Paul-Schiff, M., "Zur Statistik der Kriminalität der Juden, *Zeitschrift*, V (1909).

Peters, W., "Rassenpsychologie," in Rasse und Geist, 1932.

Peterselie, E., Untersuchungen über die Kriminalität in der Provinz Sachsen. Stuttgart, 1904.

Pittard, Eugène, Les Races et l'histoire. 1924.

——— Race and History. New York, 1926.

Ploetz, A., "Sozialanthropologie," in *Anthropologie*, Teil III, Abt. V, Die Kultur der Gegenwart, Leipzig and Berlin, 1923.

Pötsch, W., Die Judische Rasse im Lichte der Straffälligheit. Ratibor, 1932.

Praag, A. van, "De Joden en de Criminaliteit," *De Joodsche Gids*, III (1930).

Prinzing, "Soziale Faktoren der Kriminalität," *Zeitschrift für d. ges. Strafrechtswissenschaft*, XXII.

Proal, L., Le Crime et la Peine. Paris, 1894.

——— Passion and Criminality in France. Paris, 1901.

——— Political Crime. New York, 1898.

Quetelet, A., Physique sociale, II, Brussels, 1869.

Raumer, K., Raüber und Raubsituationen. Leipzig, 1937.

Reinhardt, J. M., "The Negro: Is He a Biological Inferior?" *American Journal of Sociology*, XXXIII (1927–28).

Résumé statistique de l'Empire du Japon, yearly since 1887.

Reynolds, C. H., "The Chinese Tongs," *American Journal of Sociology*, XL (1934–35).

Ripley, W. Z., The Races of Europe, New York, 1899; London, 1900.

Robison, S. M., "The Apparent Effects of the Factors of Race and Nationality on the Registration of Behavior as Delinquents in New York City in 1930," *Publications of the American Sociological Society*, XXVIII (1934).

Roos, J. R. B. de, Inleiding tot de Beoefening der Crimineele Aetiologie. Haarlem, 1908.

—— "Ueber die Kriminalität der Juden," *Monatsschrift*, VI (1909–10).

Root, W. T., Jr., A Psychological and Educational Survey of 1,916 Prisoners in the Western Penitentiary of Pennsylvania. Pittsburgh, 1927.

Royer, Clémence, Discussion sur "Les Dernières Recherches d'Anthropologie Criminelle," *Actes du IIme Congrès International d'Anthropologie Criminelle* (1890).

Ruppin, Arthur, The Jews in the Modern World. London, 1934.

—— "Die Kriminalität der Christen und Juden in Deutschland, 1899–1902," *Zeitschrift*, I (1905).

—— Soziologie der Juden, I, Berlin, 1930.

Schaaf, Gertrud, Ueber die Besonderheiten des jüdischen Geistes und ihre Ursachen. Heidelberg, 1933.

Scheidt, Walter, Allgemeine Rassenkunde. Munich, 1925.

Schmoller, Gustav, Grundriss der allgemeine Volkswirtschaftslehre. Munich, 1923.

Segall, J., "Die Kriminalität der Juden in Deutschland während der Jahre 1915 and 1916 in Vergleich mit der Vorkriegszeit," *Zeitschrift*, N.F. I (1924).

Sellin, T., "The Negro Criminal; a Statistical Note," *Annals of The American Academy of Political and Social Science*, CXXX (1928).

Slingenberg, J., "Coloration capillaire et criminalite," *2d Session de l'Institut International d'Anthropologie,* Prague, 1924; Paris, 1926.

Sombart, Werner, Die Juden und das Wirtschaftsleben. Leipzig, 1911.

—— The Jews and Modern Capitalism. New York, 1914.

Statistisches Material der kriminalbiologischen Sammelstelle des bayerischen Staates, Bericht, I, Straubing, 1926.

Steinmetz, S. R., "Der erbliche Rassen- und Volkscharacter," in *Gesammelte kleinere Schriften zur Ethnologie und Soziologie,* II, Groningen, 1928–35.

S. R. Steinmetz, J. A. J. Barge, A. L. Hagedoorn, and R. Steinmetz, De Rassen der Menschheid, 1938.

Stoffelt, "A Study of National and Cultural Difference in Criminal Tendency, *Archives of Psychology,* No. 185 (1935).

Stöwesand, W., Die Kriminalität in der Provinz Posen und ihre Ursachen. Stuttgart, 1910.

Suermondt, G. L., "De criminaliteit onder de Joden," *Tijdschrift,* XXXIII (1923).

Sutherland, E. H., Criminology. Philadelphia and London, 1924.

Taft, D. R., "Nationality and Crime," *American Sociological Review,* I (1936).

Tarde, Gabriel, La Philosophie pénale. Paris, 1903.

—— Penal Philosophy. Boston, 1912.

Tarnowski, E., "La delinquenza e la vita sociale in Russie," *Rivista Italiana di Sociologia,* II (1898).

—— "Le Mouvement de la criminalité en Russie," *Archives,* XIII (1898).

—— "Répartition géographique de la criminalité en Russie," *Archives,* XVI (1901).

Thon, J., "Die Kriminalität der Christen und Juden in Oesterreich, *Zeitschrift,* II (1906).

—— "Kriminalität der Christen und Juden in Ungarn im Jahre 1904, *Zeitschrift,* II, 1906 (or III, 1907?).

Travaglino, "De schizophrenie en de Javaansche psyche," *Psychiatrische en Neurologische Bladen,* XXXI (1927).

Tschisch, W., "La Criminalité comparée des Estes et des Lettoniens," (*Compte rendu du Vme Congrès International d'Anthropologie Criminelle*, Amsterdam, 1901).

United States. Bureau of the Census, Prisoners and Juvenile Delinquents in the United States, 1910. Washington, 1918.

United States. Federal Bureau of Investigation, Uniform Crime Reports for the United States and Its Possessions, Washington, 1938.

Urbye, A. T., "Kriminalität und Rechtspflege in nördlichsten Norwegen," *Zeitschrift für die gesammte Strafrechtswissenschaft*, XXXII (1911).

Verkko, V., "Eine Untersuchung über die ethnischen Verscheidenheiten der Gewaltkriminalität mit besonderer Berücksichtigung des Alkoholgenusses" (summary of a book published in Finnish in 1936, arranged by K. Helasvuo, with the author). *Monatsschrift für Kriminalpsychologie und Strafrechtsreform*, XXIX, 1938.

—— Verbrechen wider das Leben und Körperverletzungsverbrechen, Helsinki, 1937.

Vervaeck, L., Syllabus du Cours d'Anthropologie Criminelle, Brussels, 1926.

Villamor, I., "Propensity to Crime," *Journal of the American Institute of Criminal Law and Criminology*, VI (1915–16).

Vitcles, M. S., "The Mental Status of the Negro," *Annals of the American Academy of Political and Social Science*, CXXX (1928).

Washington, Booker T., "Negro Crime and Strong Drink," *Journal*, III (1912–13).

Wassermann, R., "Beruf, Konfession, und Verbrechen," München, 1907.

—— "Ist die Kriminalität der Juden Rassenkriminalität?" *Zeitschrift*, VII (1911).

—— "Kriminalität der Juden," *Judisches Lexikon*, III (1929).

—— "Die Kriminalität der Juden in Deutschland in den Letzten 25 Jahren (1882–1906), *Monatsschrift*, VI (1909–10).

Wassermann, R., "Kritische und ergänzende Bemerkungen über die Kriminalität der Juden," *Zeitschrift*, II (1906).

—— "Kritische und ergänzende Bemerkungen zur neuen Literatur über die Kriminalität der Juden," *Zeitschrift*, IV (1908).

—— "Zur Theorie und Methode der Kriminalstatistik," *Monatsschrift*, VI (1909–10).

Weber, Max, Gesammelte Aufsätze zur Religionssoziologie, 1920.

—— The Protestant Ethic and the Spirit of Capitalism, London, 1930.

Weidenreich, F., "Die physischen Grundlagen der Rassenlehre," in Rasse und Geist, Leipzig, 1932.

Weinberg, R., "Psychische Degeneration, Kriminalität, und Rasse," *Monatsschrift für Kriminalpsychologie*, II (1906).

Wigmore, J. H., A Preliminary Bibliography of Modern Criminal Law and Criminology, Chicago, 1909.

Willemse, W. A., Constitution-types in Delinquency, London, 1932.

—— The Road to the Reformatory, Pretoria, S.A., 1938.

Willemse, W. A., and C. I. Rademeyer, Kriminologie, Pretoria, S.A., 1933.

Work, M. N., A Bibliography of the Negro in Africa and America, New York, 1928.

—— "Crime among the Negroes of Chicago," (*American Journal*, VI, 1900–01).

—— "Negro Criminality in the South," *Annals of the American Academy of Political and Social Science*, XLIX (1913).

Wulffen, E., Kriminalpsychologie, Berlin, 1926.

—— Der Sexualverbrecher, Berlin, Gross-Lichterfelde, 1910.

—— Psychologie des Verbrechers I., Gross-Lichterfelde, Ost, 1908.

Wulfften-Palthe, P. M. van., "Forensische psychiatrie in Nederlands-Indië," *Verslagen van het Psychiatrisch-Juridisch Geselschap*, No. 18 (1936).

Wulfften-Palthe, P. M. van., "Geestesstoornis en Gemeenschaps-structuur," *Geneeskundig Tijdschrift voor Nederland Indië*, LXXVI (1936).

Wundt, W. M., Elements of Folk Psychology, New York, 1916.

—— Völkerpsychologie, VII, 1917, Leipzig, 1900–1920.

Zollschan, I., Das Rassenproblem, 2d ed. (1911).

—— The Significance of the Racial Factor as a Basis in Cultural Development, London, 1934.

For recent works on race, see: Barzun, Jacques, *Race: a Study of Modern Superstition* (with extensive critical bibliography), New York, 1937; Schwesinger, G. C., *Heredity and Environment* (with large bibliography including most references up to 1933), New York, 1933.

—Translator's note

Index

Africa, North, 36; South, 37
Age, relation to crime, 51, 75
Aggressive crime, *see* Crime
Alcoholism, 46, 61, 82, 93-96, *passim*, 102
Algerians, 37
Alpines, 66; race mixture, 39, 41; case studies, 76-86; where found, 76; characteristics, 76, 84; criminality difficult to determine, 76-80; causes of criminality, 80-83; psychical disposition, 83-86
Americas, the, 40; *see also* United States
Amir, M., on Indonesia, 33
Ammon, early anthropologist, 8
Ammoun, Fouad, on Syria, 36
Anthropology, a natural science, 1n; definition and theories of race, 1-3; views of early anthropologists, 8; views of Italian school, 18; criminal-anthropological thought in Nazi Germany, 24, 25; studies on race mixtures, 41; characteristics of Mediterraneans, 67; Alpines, 76; Nordics, 86; East Baltics, 97-102; conclusions of no significance for criminology, 103
Antisocial inclinations, ascendency over restraints, 28
Anutschine, quoted by Lombroso, 18
Arabs, 19, 36, 37
Arène, S., on Arabs in Tunis, 37
Army tests, 16, 50
Arrii, D. C., on Algerians, 37
Aschaffenburg, G., 24n, 61, 63, 80n, 82; quoted, 21, 100
Aspö Islands, 19

Aurignac man, 20
Austria, 19, 52-53, 79, 82
Avé-Lallement, F. C. B., 59n

Balkans, 67n, 68, 69
Barge, J. A. J., 36; defines race, 2; on spiritual variations in races, 7
Beach, W. G., on crimes of Orientals in California, 31
Belgium, 19, 76, 81, 86
Berbers, 37
Bertholon, Lucien, study on Tunis, 37
Bessler, K., 101
Beta tests, 51
Bijlmer, H. J. T., on New Guinea (Papuans), 5
Biology, meaning of "race" in, 3n
Bio-sociological writers who have considered race and crime relationship, 21 ff.
Black race, 3, 10, 104; *see also* Negroes
Blonds, temperament, 90
Boas, Franz, 11, 41; on structure of brain, 9
Bonger, Adriaan, 56, 68, 77; definition of crime, 27; table from his *Geloof en misdaad*, 56; table from his *Criminality and Economic Conditions*, 68; table from his "Misdaad en socialisme," 77
Boule, Marcellin, definition of race, 1
Bournet, A., on crime in France, 70
Brachycephalic people, 8
Brain, relation between intellect and brain capacity, 8 f.; of whites and Negroes, 9n
Brazil, 40

California, crimes of Orientals in, 31

Case studies, Negroes, 42-51; Jews, 51-66; Mediterraneans, 66-75; Alpines, 76-86; Nordics, 86-90; Ugro-Finns, 90-97; East Baltics and others, 97-102

Caste system, effect upon Negroes, 46-47

Catholics, *see* Roman Catholics

Caucasus, 98

Chamberlain, Houston S., 10

Character, relation to, of intelligence, 17; of criminality, 26; research in, 104

Chinese, 30, 32; in United States, 30

Colajanni, N., 21, 71

Commercial crimes, of Jews, 53, 57, 59 f.

Commercial life, Jews in, 59 f.

Constitution types, 6n

Corre, Armand, on race and crime, 22 ff.; on Chinese, 30; on mixed parentage, 39

Corsica, 70, 71

Cranial capacity, 8

Creoles, 22n

Crime and criminality, Lombroso quoted on, 18; types of, influenced by temperament, 23; dependent on the character of a people, 26; defined: not a characteristic, 27; diminution of, 30, 32, 73, 86; aggressive and sexual, run parallel with cultural level, 52, 72; economic, 52, 57, 59 f., 67; direct study possible only in two cases, 66; aggressive, 73, 106; whether temperament, sensuality, and age are factors in, 75; contradiction, and agreement, between criminological and psychological facts, 106; predisposition for, denied, 107 f.

Criminal statistics, throw little light on race-crime differences, 29 ff.;

case studies from (*q.v.*), 42-102; limited to white races and U.S. Negroes, 104

Crossbreeding, 4, 38, 39-41, 66

Dark-skinned races, 3, 10, 29-38, 104; *see also* Negroes

Deniker, Joseph, 2, 3; defines "race," 1, 7

Denmark, 70

Dinaric race, 67n

Dishonesty, not congenital, 106

Dolichocephalic people, 8

Dowd, Jerome, on the Negro, 51

Duynstee, W. J. A. J., on criminality of Catholics, 83

East-Baltics and others, case studies, 97-102

Economic conditions, as cause of crime, 67, 80

Egypt, 36

Emotionality, 33, 64, 85, 102

English, the, 29, 86, 90

Environment, *see* Social milieu

Esthonians, 91, 92, 96

Ethnic element, 23

European races, prehistoric, 20; types existing today, 20, 67; Indonesians compared with, 32, 34 f.; case studies: Jews, 51-66; Mediterraneans, 66-75; Alpines, 76-86; Nordics, 86-90; Ugro-Finns, 90-97; East-Baltics and others, 97-102

Exner, F., on Germany, 26, 83; on Poland, 101

Feber, G. H. A., 57n

Fellahs, 36

Ferri, Enrico, 19

Filipinos, 32

Finns, *see* Ugro-Finns

Fischer, E., on Mediterraneans, 74; opinion criticized, 75

Forel, Auguste, 64

Fouillée, Alfred, on Negroes, 49
France, 10, 19, 66, 70, 76
Fraud, Jewish record, 52, 59, 65

Galle, J., on the Polish, 100
Garofalo, R., 19
Garth, T. R., 16; on the Negro, 50, 51
Gault, R. H., on Alpine race, 84
Germany, 19, 22, 26, 51-52, 59, 80, 81, 82, 86, 99, 100 f.; Nazi race doctrine, 10, 24, 25; differences in crime among groups, 47, 48
Giardini, G., 71; on Italians, 72
Gobineau, J. A., 10, 41
Goethe, quoted, 17
Goetz, W. W., 11
Grant, Madison, 10, 41
Guégo, Henry, 70
Günther, H. F., 10, 41, 74, 84, 85; quoted, 25

Hacker, Erwin, 61, 69
Hankins, F. H., 11, 51
Hayner, N. S., 32; on Orientals in America, 30
Hentig, Hans von, on the Negro, 49; on the Poles, 101
Hersch, L., 53, 61
Hertz, F. O., 11
Herz, H., 54, 61, 79; on crime in Austria, 82
Heymans and Wiersma, 64
Historians, and their theories, 10 f., 12
History of criminology, 18-27
Hollanders, 90
Houzé, Emile, 11
Hungary, 53, 54

Inclinations, elementary, 28, 29
Indians, British, 35, 37
Indonesia, 32 ff.
Inherent qualities, 13, 18, 103; intelligence, 50-51; differences of Jews, 65

Inheritance, 3, 18, 20, 29, 104
Insult, 53, 63
Intellectualism, of Jews, 60, 62 f., 65; crimes, 52
Intelligence, relation to cranial capacity, 8; to brain quality, 9; to character, 17; as factor in crime, 17, 65; inherent, 51
Intelligence tests, 16, 50, 63
International Criminal Anthropological Congress, 20, 39, 78, 90
Italian, or Anthropological, School, 18
Italians, 19, 22, 69, 70, 71; in U.S., 70, 71, 73

Japan, *Résumé statistique de l'Empire du Japon*, 31
Japanese, 31; in United States, 31
Jhering, Rudolf von, 60*n*
Jennings, H. S., quoted by Garth, 12
Jews, a group, not a race, 38; case studies, 51-66; nature and causes of crime, 52-62, 106; women, 55, 58; young people, 53, 58, 61; occupations, 59 f., 65; psychical race factor, 62-66; nervous cases, 64, 106

Kappers, Arriëns, 9*n*
Klaatsch, Hermann, his hypothesis, 20
Klineberg, O., 50, 51; on aggressiveness, 73
Klossovsky, 91
Kocher, A., on the Arabs, 36
Kohlbrugge, J. H. F., 34
Kolaly, M. El, on Egypt, 36
Kretschmer, Ernest, 6, 33, 41, 90; quoted, 74, 83
Kurella, H., 19

Lacassagne, 36
Languages, all races can learn, 4

Lapouge, Vacher de, 8, 10
Lapps, 91
Leers, Johann von, 59*n*
Lellep, C., 93, 95; on Esthonians, 92
Lenz, F., 24, 89
Letts, 91, 96*n*
Leydesdorff, J., on the psychology of the Jews, 64, 65
Liszt, F. von, 61
Litten, K., 83
Lombroso, C., 20, 48, 49, 71; considered race significant, 18; on the Negro, 48
Loon, F. H. van, 32, 35; on Malaysians, 33

Mac Auliffe, 6
Malaysians, 33, 34
Man, physical: and as a social being, 1*n*
Mania, 24, 33
Manouvrier, L., 11
Martin, R., 25; on Hessians, 26
Marx, Karl, 59*n*, 60*n*
Mayr, Georg von, 35, 51
Mediterranean, races on east and south shores, 36
Mediterraneans, 12; case studies, 66-75; characteristics, 67, 74; where found, 67; nature and extent of crimes, 68-71, 106; causes, 71-74; in U.S., 70 f.; psychological study of, 74 f.; temperament, 106
Melancholia, 24, 33
Mezger, Edmond, 25
Mikorey, M., 59*n*
Milieu, *see* Social milieu
Mok, S., 58
Mongolian race, 29-32
Monogenic theory of race origin, 2
Müller-Lyer, F. C., 13

Naecke, P., 40; on variations among races, 23
Neanderthal man, 20
Negroes, brains of whites and, 8,

9*n*; in South Africa, 37; case studies, United States, 38, 42-51, 104; nature of crimes, 43 f.; social influences, 43, 45 ff.; causes of greater criminality among, 45; psychology, 47-50
Nervous type, 64, 106
Netherlands, 13, 77 f., 82, 83, 86, 87; Jews in, 56-59, 61, 64, 66
Nietzsche, Friedrich W., 89
Nieuwenhuis, A. W., on Malaysians, 34
Nina-Rodrigues, Raymundo, on Brazil, 39
Nordics, 10, 12, 22, 24, 25, 26, 75, 84, 91, 92, 96*n*, 106; race mixture, 39, 41; case studies, 86-90; where found, 86; characteristics, 86, 89; slight criminality, 86; reasons, 88; psychical disposition, 88-90
Norway, 86*n*, 91, 92

Occupational criminality, 60
Oppenheimer, Franz, 11
Orientals, 29-32

Papuans, dwarf, 5
Peters, W., 16, 51; quoted, 13
Peterselie, E., 101
Philippines, 32
Phlegmatic type, 107
Pittard, Eugéne, 1, 11
Ploetz, A., 24
Poland, Jews in, 55; Russian Poland, 98; murder in, 100
Poles, case studies, 99-102; races, 99
Polygenic theory of race origin, 2
Predisposition to crime, 29, 107 f.
Prehistoric races, 20
Primitive peoples, 5, 8, 15*n*, 72
Protestants, statistics on crime among, 56, 57, 58
Psychiatrists, studies by, 32 ff.
Psychical disposition of races, 5 ff.; historians and their theories, 10 f.,

12; psychical changeableness in a single race: attitude of sociologists, 12; Negroes, 47-50; Jews, 62-66; Mediterraneans, 74 f.; Alpines, 83-86; Nordics, 88-90
Psychology, race, 14-17, 103; importance of American investigations, 16; scientific, 104; contradiction, and agreement, between criminological and psychological facts, 106
Psychopathic differences, 23 f., 33
Psychoses, organic, 34
Pugnacity, Nordic, 89

Quetelet, A., 70

Race, defined, 1-3; racial mixture, 4, 38, 39-41, 66; psychical disposition, 5 ff., 12; connection between physical build and character, 6; race psychology, 14-17; opinions on differences in, 23; races which may be studied directly: indirectly, 66; differences that may be taken as positive, 105
Race and crime, history of connection, 18-27; importance of race in the etiology of crime? 24, 82; theoretical consideration of connection between, 27-41; case studies (Negroes, 41-51; Jews, 51, 52-66; Mediterraneans, 66-75; Alpines, 76-86; Nordics, 86-90; Ugro-Finns, 90-97; East Baltics and others, 97-102; why no definite conclusions reached, 103 ff.; differences and changes in criminality within one race, 107; see also Crime and criminality; Social milieu
Rademeyer, C. I., and W. A. Willemse, on South Africa, 37
Restraints, 28, 29
Ripley, W. Z., 11, 67, 84, 90

Roman Catholics, 83; criminal statistics for, 56, 57, 58
Romance people, 24
Roos, J. R. B. de, 61; on the Jews, 62
Root, W. T., Jr., on the Negro, 46
Royer, Clémence, 39
Ruppin, Arthur, on the Jews, 63
Russia, 18, 40; East Baltics and others, 97-99

Scandinavian peoples, 86n, 90-97
Scottish, 86n
Segall, J., 53
Sensuality: of Tunisians, 37; of Negroes, 50, 75; of Jews, 65
Sexual crime, see Crime
Slavic peoples, 19, 24, 99n, 101
Slingenberg, J., 78, 82
Social milieu, influence upon talents, 13; could influence be eliminated in experiments, 15; upon temperament, 15n, 29, 104; influence upon crime, 22, 30, 33, 67, 71, 80, 82; theory supported by French criminologists, 22; influence upon inclination and restraints, 29; milieu-as-cause theory of crime, 33; influence of milieu upon Negroes in United States, 43, 45 ff.; upon Jews, 59; the decisive factor in diminution of aggressive crime, 73; need of research to separate inheritance from, 104
Sociologists, and their theories, 12, 21
Sombart, Werner, 62, 63
Spain, 19, 71
Species, as distinguished from race, 2
Statistics, see Criminal statistics
Steinmetz, S. R., 7, 11, 15n, 63
Stone Age men, 5, 6
Stöwesand, W., on the Poles, 100
Subraces, crossbreeding among, 4

Suermondt, G. L., 61
Sutherland, E. H., on Italians in
America, 73; on the Negro, 46
Syria, 36

Talents, variability, 12; influence of
environment, 13
Tarnowski, E., 97
Temperament, influence of environment, 15*n*, 29, 104; investigations concerning, 16; connection between race, types of crime,
and, 23, 75, 106 f.; do races differ
in? 28; Jewish, 64; Nordic, 90; research in, 104
Theoretical consideration of connection between race and crime,
27-41
Thon, J., 54
Tschisch, W., 90; on Esthonians
and Letts, 93
Tunis, 36, 37

Ugro-Finns, case studies, 90-97; divergent criminality, 91; explained,
93-96; influence of race, 95-97
United States, doctrine of white su-
periority, 10; investigations in
race psychology, 16; Orientals in,
30-32; Negroes, 38, 42-51, 104 (*see
entries under* Negroes); caste system, 46; Italians in, 70, 71, 73;
other immigrants, 70, 87, 93, 99
Urbye, A. T., 91, 93; on Finns, 92

Variability, psychical, within one
race, 12
Vendetta, 36, 37
Verkko, V., 92-96, 98, 99, 101; on
Finns, 94
Viernstein, 24
Villamor, L., 32*n*
Viteles, M. S., 50, 51

Wagemann, 25
Wassermann, R., 59, 61
Weber, Max, 13; quoted, 14
Weidenreich, F., definition of race,
1; on spiritual qualities of races,
7; on the brain, 9
Weinberg, R., 40, 93; on Esthonians
and Letts, 91
White race, 3, 10; comparison with
Negroes, 9*n*, 37, 42-51; racial mix-
ture in Europe, 38, 39-41; crim-
inal statistics limited to, 104
Wiersma, Heymans and, 64
Willemse, W. A., and Rademeyer,
C. F., on South Africa, 37
Woltmann, 10
Women, gypsy, 19; Jewish, 55, 58
Wulffen, E., 64
Wulfften-Palthe, P. M. van, 34
Wundt, W. M., 5

Yellow race, 3, 29-32, 104

Zollschan, I., 63